Number Three: The Montague History of Oil Series

Early Louisiana and Arkansas Oil

Drilling in Catahoula Lake, St. Martin Parish, in 1930 or 1931. The platform technique being used was employed throughout Louisiana for near-shore drilling in lakes, bayous, and coastal waters along the Gulf of Mexico. The platform contains the steam boiler and also storage tanks. The small boat in the foreground was used to transport workers to and from the well. *Louisiana State Library*.

Early Louisiana and Arkansas Oil

A Photographic History, 1901-1946

By KENNY A. FRANKS

and PAUL F. LAMBERT

TEXAS A&M UNIVERSITY PRESS   College Station

Library of Congress Cataloging in Publication Data

Franks, Kenny Arthur, 1945–
    Early Louisiana and Arkansas oil.

    (The Montague history of oil series   ; no. 3)
    Bibliography: p.
    Includes index.
    1. Petroleum industry and trade—Louisiana—His-
    tory—20th century. 2. Petroleum industry and trade—
    Arkansas—History—20th century. I. Lambert, Paul F.
    II. Title. III. Series.
    HD9567.L8F72 1982   338.2′7282′09763   82-40313
    ISBN 0-89096-134-4(cloth); ISBN 0-89096-990-6(pbk.)

Contents

Preface

WHILE this is not a definitive study of the petroleum industry of Louisiana and Arkansas, it does pull together much of the scattered information concerning the oil development of the two states. Unlike their sister states in the Mid-Continent or Gulf Coast regions, Louisiana and Arkansas have had little historical research into their oil heritage. This void of information has left a great gap to be filled, as the two states were among the nation's leading oil producers.

Although much material relating to individual wells and pools is included in this book, the authors have not deviated from the basic task of a pictorial history: providing a visual tour through the entire panorama of the oil-boom age.

The petroleum legacy of Louisiana and Arkansas predated the exploration of the area by whites, and by the time of Colonel E. L. Drake's well at Titusville, Pennsylvania (1859), Louisiana's oil seeps were well known and valuable sources of tar for the caulking of ships. Many early attempts were made to tap the region's rich deposits of crude, but all failed. Finally, in 1901, W. Scott Heywood and S. A. Spencer opened Louisiana's huge Jennings Field, and the rush was on. Two decades later, on January 10, 1921, the Busey No. 1 blew in near El Dorado, Arkansas, and began that state's oil boom. Eventually the two states became the center of one of the wildest oil stampedes ever—one in which oil men braved thick forests, almost impenetrable swamps, and the open sea to pull the crude from the earth.

Because the booms of Louisiana and Arkansas started at the beginning of the twentieth century, their oil scenes were vividly recorded by the camera. Through a careful search for all available photographs, we have attempted to present a realistic account of one of America's greatest oil rushes—a boom which in many ways revolutionized the world's petroleum industry through the development of new drilling techniques that opened vast new horizons to development.

Acknowledgments

THE cooperation of many people was required to make *Early Louisiana and Arkansas Oil* possible. Without the editing expertise of Dr. Odie B. Faulk, this book would not have been possible. In addition, were it not for the photographic assistance and moral support of Judy Lambert, we would have found it impossible to complete the task. The typing of Harriet Mowery was also indispensable.

Among those helping with the accumulation of photographs and the securing of research materials were Thomas R. Barton, Lafayette, Louisiana, formerly Executive Director of the Louisiana Association of Independent Producers and Royalty Owners; S. K. ("Ken") Childers, Phillips Petroleum Company, Bartlesville, Oklahoma; Peggy Coe, Oklahoma Department of Libraries, Oklahoma City; Robert L. Dodson, Camden, Arkansas; Dan Droege, Phillips Petroleum Company, Bartlesville, Oklahoma; Lynn Eubanks, Arkansas History Commission, Little Rock; Bob Finney, Phillips Petroleum Company, Bartlesville, Oklahoma; Karen Fite, Oklahoma Department of Libraries, Oklahoma City; Gary Hacking, Executive Director, Arkansas Oil Heritage Center, Smackover; Mary Hardin, Oklahoma Department of Libraries, Oklahoma City; Max Hebert, Texaco, Inc., New Orleans; J. Marshall Jones, Jr., Shreveport; James O. Kemm, Executive Manager, Oklahoma Petroleum Council, Tulsa; Eugene Spruell, Shreveport; John Steiger, Historical Consultant for Cities Service Oil Company, Tulsa; and Mary Sweeney, Oklahoma Department of Libraries, Oklahoma City.

Others who provided photographs and assistance were Shelly Arlen, Western History Collections, University of Oklahoma, Norman; Mrs. Claude V. Barrow, Oklahoma City; Jack Haley, Western History Collections, University of Oklahoma, Norman; Harriett Cale, Sandel Library, Northeast Louisiana State University, Monroe; Harriett Callahan, Louisiana State Library, Baton Rouge; Jack Crichton, Dallas, Texas; Richard Drew, American Petroleum Institute, Washington, D.C.; W. B. Grabill, Shreveport; J. Marshall Jones, Sr., Shreveport; P. C. Lauinger, Sr., PennWell Publishing Company, Tulsa; Gisela Lozada, Louisiana State Library Staff, Baton Rouge; Patricia L. Meador, Louisiana

State University at Shreveport; Jack Norman, Vivian, Louisiana; C. R. Pope, Lafayette, Louisiana; Graydon F. Smart, Editor-Manager, *Shreveport Magazine*; Ron Shultz, Jennings, Louisiana; and Irma Tucker, Baton Rouge.

Photographs and information also were provided by the Arkansas History Commission staff, Little Rock; the Jennings Carnegie Public Library staff, Jennings, Louisiana; the Zigler Museum staff, Jennings, Louisiana; and the Interstate Oil Compact Commission staff, Oklahoma City.

Among the many companies that provided the authors with photographs, many of which have never before been published, were Cities Service Oil Company, Kerr-McGee Corporation, PennWell Publishing Company, Phillips Petroleum Company, Rathbourne Land Company, *Shreveport Magazine*, and Texaco, Inc.

Early Louisiana and Arkansas Oil

Introduction

LOUISIANA is a land of varied geography, its terrain ranging from bayous and coastal marshes to deltas and hills. In its 50,820 square miles can be found saltwater lagoons and lakes, tidal islands covered with sedge and rushes, a mighty river that drains the heartland of America, longleaf pines and magnolias, and bayous teeming with wildlife. Louisiana is a land rich in people, its citizens speaking a colorful mixture of Cajun French, English, and Spanish. It is a land equally rich in natural resources: salt, sulfur, fish, fertile soil, and, perhaps most important in terms of dollar value, oil and natural gas. Freebooters stalking Spanish galleons along the coast of Louisiana little realized that beneath their keels was petroleum of greater value than all the gold and silver ever taken out of the New World. Yet from the earliest records of man's tenure in rich and beautiful Louisiana there have been attempts to use that resource. Only in the twentieth century, however, would its full potential be realized.

For centuries the Indians of Louisiana used the state's natural oil springs as a source of medicine for both themselves and their animals. However, Louisiana's vast reservoir of crude oil was first discovered by non-Indians when survivors of Hernando DeSoto's ill-fated expedition passed through the region in the early 1540s. While making their way to Spanish settlements in Mexico in several small ships, the remnants of that party of explorers were struck by bad weather and driven onto the Louisiana shore on July 25, 1542. As they struggled to regroup their scattered band, they gathered their ships at a creek where they located an oil spring and used the oil, which they called stone pitch, to make their ships more watertight.

A century and one-half later, in 1698, an Englishman named Daniel Coxe led an expedition to the Gulf Coast region, and he likewise reported locating several petroleum deposits oozing from the ground. Still other early adventurers recorded a "strong smell" as they sailed along the Louisiana coast. In 1812, Major Amos Stoddard in his book on Lousiana described an island to the west of the Atchafalaya River (probably one of the Five—or Fire—Islands along Louisiana's Gulf Coast) which had burned for at least three months. Two American surveyors, James L. Cathcart and James Hutton, visited the Belle Isle region of Louisiana between 1819 and 1821 and reported a spring that burned.

As early as 1833, gas bubbles were reported rising to the surface of Bayou Bouillon in St. Martin Parish, and in 1839 the *American Journal of Science* described several oil springs along the Calcasieu and Sabine rivers. One of the springs reportedly flowed with as much as three or four barrels of crude daily. Yet before the mid-1800s, local residents found little use for Louisiana's petroleum deposits except for medicinal purposes or for lubrication of wagon wheels. However, when Edwin L. Drake brought in the first commercial oil well at Titusville, Pennsylvania, in 1859, the value of the crude became apparent. Coincidental with Drake's discovery came the development of refining techniques that allowed the use of petroleum as a source of illuminating oil.

Almost immediately there was an oil rush to Louisiana. In 1860 several pioneer oil men sent samples of the state's crude to New York City for analysis. The test results showed that Louisiana oil would be excellent for refining into kerosene, and a company was quickly formed to exploit the known oil springs in Calcasieu Parish, Louisiana. One citizen of Sulphur, Louisiana, a Dr. Kikman, sank a 450-foot well in the Calcasieu region before abandoning the hole when the drill pipe became clogged.

With the outbreak of the Civil War, the search for crude in Louisiana received a boost when Governor Henry W. Allen, in an effort to make the state self-sufficient, ordered two separate studies of the state's mineral resources. Allen appointed John B. Robertson and Charles N. Tripp to examine the state's mineral deposits and report on the oil springs of the Calcasieu region. Tripp concluded that if the petroleum deposits of the Calcasieu area alone were developed, they quickly would become the major source of oil for the entire Confederacy. The war ended, however, before Robertson completed his investigation.

Louisiana's postwar governor, J. Madison Wells, sent Robertson back to the Calcasieu area to finish the study. Robertson's report confirmed what Tripp had concluded several years earlier, suggesting that state-owned land near Calcasieu be leased to oil men and the money used to retire Louisiana's war debt.

Tripp's and Robertson's studies had not gone unnoticed. By 1866 southwestern Louisiana was a mecca for pioneer oil men. That same year, the state's first petroleum firm, the Louisiana Petroleum and Coal Oil Company, was organized. Headquartered in New Orleans, its stockholders included Judge William G. Swan, who served as president, L. A. Fournier, and I. W. Patton. In June, 1866, this firm began work on a well in the Calcasieu region on a farm owned by Hilaire Escoubas and Truxton Lowell. Though another well, drilled fifteen miles west of Lake Charles at the head of Bayou Choupique, struck an oil sand at 160 feet, no oil was found in paying quantities, and the hole was abandoned at 1,230 feet.

That same year, another petroleum firm began work on a seven-thousand-acre tract near the Louisiana Petroleum and Coal Oil Company's leases, but nothing was found.

There was a strike in north Louisiana in September, 1866, but northern businessmen were hesistant to invest in a state that had fought for the Confederacy, and there was no development of the region.

Although most oil men knew there was crude in Louisiana, it was not until 1893 that another major effort was made to exploit the finds. That year Anthony Lucas, a young mining engineer, arrived in Iberia Parish, Louisiana, to oversee the Miles and Company salt mines at Avery Island, about nine miles southeast of New Iberia. Lucas soon discovered that the deposit was a huge salt dome instead of a stratified layer of the mineral. Several exploratory drillings into the formation indicated the presence of oil.

Two years later, in 1895, Lucas moved to the salt mines at Jefferson Island, about five miles northwest of Avery Island. There he again sank several exploratory holes, proving that the formation was a huge salt dome. In addition, he found several showings of oil in the borings. Impressed with his findings, Lucas began drilling his own well in 1896 at Belle Isle, the southernmost of the Five Islands, or what Stoddard had called the Fire Islands, off Louisiana's southwestern coast. Several traces of oil were found, but a shortage of capital forced Lucas to abandon the project.

Lucas continued to search southwestern Louisiana for evidence of other salt domes, and in 1899 he started work on another well at Anse la Butte, about five miles north of Lafayette. Lucas was convinced that oil could be found in conjunction with the salt domes, but at 523 feet he once again was forced to abandon the hole when he ran out of money. Discouraged, he moved to Beaumont, Texas, where in January, 1901, he discovered the huge Spindletop Field.

The discovery at Beaumont sparked another round of oil fever in Louisiana. Oil men invaded the areas where Lucas previously had found signs of petroleum. It was only a matter of time before a discovery would be made and touch off a Louisiana oil boom, and the find came in September, 1901, at Jennings in the same general region of southwestern Louisiana where Escoubas and Lowell had searched four decades previously and where Lucas had given up after going broke.

The oil boom triggered by the find at Jennings pushed Louisiana into the forefront of the nation's oil-producing areas. From 1901 through 1946, Louisiana produced 1,949,819,000 barrels of crude from such fields as Jennings, Caddo, Homer, and Cotton Valley. Throughout that period the state ranked no lower than eighth among the oil-producing states, and on several occasions it rose as high as third.

Eventually the search for crude in northern Louisiana spilled over into southern Arkansas. Such names as El Dorado, Smackover, and Magnolia were quickly added to the list of producing fields. Although the Arkansas boom did not get underway until the early 1920s, that state produced 703,326,000 barrels of petroleum, enough to rank Arkansas fourth among the nation's oil-producing states in 1923, 1925, and 1926.

LOUISIANA PRODUCTION, 1902–1947

Year	Barrels Produced Annually	Average Price* North	Average Price* Gulf Coast	Rank among Oil-Producing States
1902	549,000		$0.34	8th
1903	918,000		.45	8th
1904	2,959,000		.36	8th
1905	8,910,000		.18	7th
1906	9,077,000		.39	7th
1907	5,000,000	$0.81	.81	9th
1908	5,789,000	.60	.62	8th
1909	3,060,000	.66	.72	8th
1910	6,841,000	.52	.73	8th
1911	10,721,000	.53	.54	4th
1912	9,263,000	.76	.77	6th
1913	12,499,000	1.00	.90	5th
1914	14,309,000	.95	.67	5th
1915	18,192,000	.62	.46	5th
1916	15,248,000	1.03	.73	5th
1917	11,392,000	1.64	1.11	6th
1918	16,043,000	1.73	1.64	5th
1919	17,118,000	1.62	1.17	5th
1920	35,174,000	3.19	2.14	5th
1921	27,103,000	1.60	1.16	5th
1922	35,376,000	1.52	1.25	4th
1923	24,919,000	1.48	1.46	7th
1924	21,124,000	1.41	1.63	7th
1925	20,272,000	1.61	1.57	7th
1926	23,201,000	1.70	1.39	6th
1927	22,818,000	1.33	1.21	6th
1928	21,847,000	1.20	1.16	6th
1929	20,554,000	1.26	1.23	6th
1930	23,272,000	1.15	1.07	5th
1931	21,804,000	.64	.67	5th
1932	21,807,000	.90	.81	5th
1933	25,168,000	.58	.63	5th
1934	32,869,000	.93	.98	5th
1935	50,330,000	.94	1.00	5th
1936	80,491,000	1.07	1.06	4th
1937	90,924,000	1.19	1.22	4th
1938	95,208,000	1.15	1.16	4th

*Per 42-U.S. Gallon Barrel

1939	93,646,000	1.01	1.06	5th
1940	103,584,000	1.00	1.05	5th
1941	115,908,000	1.18	1.13	5th
1942	115,785,000	1.20	1.19	4th
1943	123,592,000	1.21	1.22	4th
1944	129,645,000	1.21	1.23	3rd
1945	131,051,000	1.20	1.24	4th
1946	143,669,000	1.43	1.45	3rd
1947	160,128,000	1.99	2.01	3rd

ARKANSAS OIL PRODUCTION, 1921–1947

Year	Barrels Produced Annually	Average Price*	Rank among Oil-Producing States
1921	10,473,000	$1.22	7th
1922	12,712,000	1.61	8th
1923	36,610,000	.69	4th
1924	46,028,000	.94	5th
1925	77,398,000	.89	4th
1926	58,332,000	1.11	4th
1927	40,005,000	1.06	5th
1928	32,096,000	.86	5th
1929	24,917,000	.88	5th
1930	19,702,000	.88	6th
1931	14,791,000	.49	7th
1932	12,051,000	.64	7th
1933	11,686,000	.42	6th
1934	11,182,000	.72	8th
1935	11,008,000	.72	9th
1936	10,469,000	.78	9th
1937	11,764,000	.97	9th
1938	18,180,000	.93	9th
1939	21,238,000	.79	9th
1940	25,775,000	.84	7th
1941	26,327,000	.93	8th
1942	26,628,000	.99	9th
1943	27,600,000	.99	8th
1944	29,418,000	1.05	8th
1945	28,613,000	1.07	8th

*Per 42-U.S. Gallon Barrel

ARKANSAS OIL PRODUCTION, 1921–1947

Year	Barrels Produced Annually	Average Price*	Rank among Oil-Producing States
1946	28,375,000	1.26	8th
1947	29,948,000	1.82	9th

Within forty-five years of the beginning of production at Jennings, the oil area of Louisiana and southern Arkansas would produce billions of dollars' worth of crude. In 1947 the two states had a total of 12,290 producing wells—3,590 in Arkansas, 4,790 in northern Louisiana, and 3,910 along Louisiana's Gulf Coast. Their average daily output of 140 barrels of crude per well totaled 1,720,600 barrels of oil every twenty-four hours, with the highest average daily production—190.3 barrels per well—coming from the Gulf Coast. Throughout the boom era, between 1901 and 1947, Louisiana and Arkansas produced crude worth $3,202,912,000. Then, just as the first boom ended in 1947, a second started with completion of the first offshore well out of sight of land, an innovation that opened an entirely new frontier of oil exploration and production to oil men.

This well, somewhere in northern Louisiana, required fifteen cords of wood each day when operating at maximum load. The boiler pit shown has a three-day supply of water for the steam boiler. This particular well also featured an electric lighting system. *W. B. Grabill.*

Three gentlemen with "an instrument for locating oil." These men apparently sold the services of their oil-finding machine in northern Louisiana and southern Arkansas, but the extent of the success they enjoyed with this suspicious-looking gadget has been lost to history. *Graydon F. Smart, Shreveport Magazine.*

Open-pit storage was frequently used throughout Arkansas and Louisiana as the massive production of many fields exceeded facilities for storage and transportation of the product. Here, oil is flowing through five pipes from an Otto, Morris, and Myrr well into a new earthen storage pit. *Ron Shipman Collection, Arkansas Oil Heritage Center.*

Thousands of individuals and families gained their livelihood from employment in the oil industry in Arkansas and Louisiana. These five workers take a break for the photographer. Note the use of crude logs and lumber to build the foundation of the derrick, located somewhere in the Smackover, Arkansas, Field. *Max Taylor Collection, Arkansas Oil Heritage Center.*

A drilling crew on a derrick floor at Smackover. The huge bull wheel, at the left, which during drilling held the heavy cable required to support and move the drill bit, has been left in place, though the well is now pumping. *Phillips Petroleum.*

Searching for and producing petroleum in the swamps of Louisiana often were difficult tasks, requiring extraordinary measures. Here, a crude narrow-gauge railroad was devised to transport pipe. Note the log ties and the curved rails. *PennWell Publishing Company.*

One means of getting oil-field equipment into Louisiana swamps was to construct a plank road, like this one being built by an Arkansas Fuel Oil Company crew in August, 1943. In many areas such roads provided the only means of transportation for motorized vehicles. *Cities Service.*

A fisherman and his friends walk along a plank road built to enable oil workers to reach a drilling rig in a Louisiana swamp. *Cities Service.*

Pipeline construction in the swamps and marshes of Louisiana was difficult work at best. The heavy underbrush and wet ground in this scene were typical of the conditions encountered by pipeliners. *PennWell Publishing Company.*

A scene typical of much of southern Louisiana: a wildcat well amid the Spanish moss. *PennWell Publishing Company.*

The Jennings Oil Company Clement No. 1, the discovery well of the Jennings Oil Field, being drilled on September 19, 1901. The well was completed two days later. (The original negative of the photograph split with age, causing the streak in the print.) Note the horses and wagon on the right used to haul supplies to the well and the casing pipe for the well on the ground. *Jennings Carnegie Public Library.*

JENNINGS, Louisiana, is about ninety miles east of Beaumont, Texas, where Lucas discovered the huge Spindletop oil field in January, 1901. Lucas's find touched off a search for crude along the entire Gulf Coast region. As word of the tremendous wealth found at Beaumont spread among residents at Jennings, many of them began to search for telltale bubbles of gas boiling up in the region's numerous bayous. Generally such a phenomenon indicated that a salt dome had pushed upward near the surface, allowing trapped gas to escape.

After the discovery at Spindletop, it was generally accepted that the salt domes of Louisiana contained oil in commercial quantities. The entire Gulf Coast area was pocked by these domelike structures formed of rock strata with a central core of rock salt. The salt had formed in the bedded rocks, and then accumulated in the porous and permeable layers of sand. As the salt plug pushed upward, it arched the beds above into dome-shaped structures. If the domed beds abutting the salt were oil-bearing formations, the oil would migrate up the slope of the beds and become trapped in the highest part of the dome. Often, in addition to oil these formations contained huge quantities of natural gas.

Dotted about the terrain along faults, the salt domes were potential sources of great wealth for early-day oil men. However, they often were isolated formations separated from one another by broad stretches of unproductive territory. Such a geographical distribution of salt domes resulted in many highly productive local pools of oil, yet scores of wells sunk "near" the oil-producing domes—in the vain hope that the crude deposits extended miles in every direction—proved to be dry. As a result, some wells drilled near the center of Louisiana's salt-dome pools were profitable producers, while other holes sunk a few hundred feet away were worthless.

It was generally known that the area around Jennings, in Jefferson Davis Parish, Louisiana, contained several gas springs. As early as April, 1893, a German homesteader had told Tom C. Mahaffey, a recent arrival in the country from the Pennsylvania oil fields, of finding a gas-emitting spring near the southwestern Louisiana community. Mahaffey, not certain that the homesteader had located a gas spring, advised the farmer to sink two two-inch holes into the formation to see how strong the gas flow was. Later the farmer returned to tell Mahaffey that the flow was strong and that he knew it was natural gas because he had set it on fire. Still unconvinced, Mahaffey contacted an Ohio oil man, told him the farmer's story, and asked his opinion. The Ohioan wrote back that it was probably nothing but marsh gas, and Mahaffey forgot the matter.

After the discovery at Spindletop, Mahaffey remembered his previous experience and persuaded some local citizens in the Jennings area—Stanley A. Spencer, Dr. A. C. Wilkins, Frank R. Jaenke, Avery C. Wilkins, and I. D. L. Williams—to join him in forming an oil exploration copartnership which they named S. A. Spencer and Company. Within a short time this company had leased nearly two thousand acres of potential oil-producing land in the vicinity of Jennings.

Among the firm's holdings were forty acres of rice land owned by Jules Clement. Located about five to six miles northeast of Jennings, just across the boundary in what then was Imperial Calcasieu Parish (later Acadia Parish), the Clement property contained several known gas seeps. It was there that Mahaffey and his partners decided to drill their first well, but first they had to acquire the necessary equipment.

In hopes of finding a driller who would join in the search, S. A. Spencer and Company sent a committee to Beaumont to talk with the Heywood Company, a Spindletop drilling firm owned by five brothers—W. Scott, Alba, O. W., Dewey, and Clint Heywood—about forming a drilling company to sink wells in the Jennings area. Intrigued by the possibility, W. Scott Heywood, the company's drilling superintendent, traveled to southwestern Louisiana to examine the Spencer and Company holdings. When he arrived at Clement's farm, however, the gates were padlocked. Clement, who had decided that any drilling effort would ruin his rice crop and that his cattle might fall into the well, had changed his mind and wanted no part of the project. Heywood attempted to calm the farmer's fears by persuading him that there was no danger of his cattle falling into the well and offering to pay him ten dollars instead of the originally agreed price of three dollars for any damage to his rice crop. When Clement still balked, Heywood promised that he would sell the farmer's share of the oil without any service charge and explained that if they were successful, Clement would be a wealthy man. At last convinced, Clement agreed to the drilling.

After visiting the site, Heywood reported back to his brothers, and they approved the Spencer and Company proposal. The Jennings Oil Company was formed with a capital of sixty thousand shares of stock valued at one dollar per share. Of this amount Spencer and Company would receive thirty thousand shares and the Heywood Company fifteen thousand shares, the remaining fifteen thousand shares to be offered for public sale. In exchange, the Heywood brothers, through their subsidiary, the Heywood Brothers & Dobbins Drilling Company, agreed to sink two wells to a depth of one thousand feet. Afterward they were to receive one-half of the lease acreage in checkerboard fashion.

Although the stock was valued at one dollar per share, the shares of public stock were sold for fifty cents each to cover the cost of the first well. Later the Heywood brothers would acquire complete control of the firm.

Little time was wasted on starting the first well. Heywood hurriedly brought to the Clement farm a draw works, a small gripping rotary, two swivels, two pumps, a forty-horsepower steam engine and boiler, several fishtail bits, and sufficient lumber and pipe to construct a sixty-four-foot derrick, and on June 15, 1901, he started work on the Jennings Oil Company Well No. 1. Elmer Dobbins, C. O. Noble, and Sank Hendricks were the drillers, and by the time the hole had penetrated 250 feet, they had found a show of oil. Unfortunately, at the 400-foot level a ten-inch piece of pipe was twisted off, forcing the drillers to move over a few feet and start again. The hole eventually reached 1,000 feet, but no other signs of oil were discovered.

Nonetheless, W. Scott Heywood believed that there was oil on the lease and that they just needed to go deeper. He succeeded in persuading Spencer and Company, which also had a contract with the same drillers to sink a 1,000-foot well on an adjacent lease once the first well was completed, to give up on the second well and allow the drilling of the Jennings No. 1 to proceed to a greater depth. Once drilling resumed, signs of oil again were found at the 1,130- and 1,400-foot levels. At once drilling stopped, the well was capped, and the gate valve was padlocked while arrangements were made for a test. Several days were required to prepare the storage tanks, but on September 21, 1901, the well was bailed, and then it came in with a four-inch stream of oil spewing higher than the derrick.

Although the Jennings Oil Company Well No. 1 flowed an estimated seven thousand barrels per day, the fine "sugar" sand of the region made it impossible to clear the hole. After the well had flowed for a while, it had piled up about a foot of sand on the derrick floor and on the rice field around the derrick. Then it suddenly stopped flowing. Resorting to the "California technique" of washing, bailing, and flushing, Heywood ran pumps day and night in an attempt to save the well. Once, for a matter of hours, the well again gushed above the derrick. But the heaving sand formation made it impossible to keep the hole clear, the well "sanded," and, after about thirty days of trying to clear it, the drillers abandoned it when a string of two-inch wash pipe became stuck in the hole.

Heywood was convinced that if he could have controlled the sand on this first well, the company would have had a well capable of flowing at a rate of at least seven thousand barrels per day. Therefore he wasted little time in starting another well near the first. During the drilling operation he had a dream in which, he later related, the problem with the sand was solved by use of a screen like those put in irrigation wells. Acting on the dream, Heywood first perforated the well piping with three-eighths-inch holes. Then he fastened some sixty-mesh gauze to the outside of the holes, forming a screen to keep out the sand. The idea proved successful, for the second well did not have the same sanding problem as had the first.

Certain that Jennings Oil Company No. 2 would be a success, Heywood laid a pipeline from the rig to the Southern Pacific Railroad terminal near Jennings. In addition, he had two storage tanks constructed: a 50,000-barrel tank near the well and a 37,500-barrel tank at the railroad loading rack. He also built a barge-loading facility on Bayou Nezpique from which the crude could be shipped to market on the Mermentau River.

The second well was brought in without clogging, but during the fall of 1902 it was struck by lightning and set afire. For nine days the blaze raged out of control. Burning oil flowed out of the hole, and Heywood had to build a huge levee around the well site to prevent flaming crude from flowing down the coulee and onto neighboring land. In an effort to put out the fire, Heywood and his brothers searched the state for the chemicals needed to extinguish the flames and hurried them to Jennings aboard special trains. A ring of twenty-two boilers was built around the burning well, and the chemicals were mixed in a nearby large pit. However, when steam from the boilers was directed at the well-head, the fire was put out without the use of the chemicals. The blaze cost nearly twenty thousand dollars to extinguish, but the well was still flowing at nearly seven thousand barrels of crude per day.

The success of these early attempts at Jennings quickly attracted several other firms to the area. Within a short time the Southern Oil Company, the Prairie Mamou Oil & Mineral Company, the Union Oil & Development Company, the Home Oil & Development Company, the Pelican Oil & Pipe Line Company, the Crowley Oil & Mineral Company, and the Spring Hill Oil Company were all active at Jennings, and other wells were quickly drilled near the original site. On six acres adjoining the Jennings No. 1, which the Heywood brothers had sold for twelve thousand dollars, a well was brought in that blew out two hundred thousand barrels of crude before it stopped gushing. In April, 1902, the Southern Oil Company completed a well flowing from the 1,830-foot level about 150 feet from the Jennings No. 1. Another well drilled by Scott Heywood was completed in June, 1902, as an initial seventy-thousand-barrel-per-day producer. That year the total production for the Jennings Field reached an estimated 548,617 barrels annually.

Within months of the completion of the first successful well, production in the Jennings Field amounted to eighty thousand barrels daily. To handle this flow, the Heywood brothers hired a contractor from Houston, Texas, to dig several earthen storage tanks nearby. Using mules and fresno scoops, the contractor excavated tanks holding from thousands to millions of barrels of oil. On moonlit winter nights, oil men had to station crews in rowboats with floodlights on the great lakes of oil to keep flocks of ducks from landing in them. Fooled by the reflection of light off the petroleum, ducks would land on the oil, become covered with crude, and die. Their remains were so dense that they clogged the intake pipes and made it impossible to ship the oil.

The growth of the Jennings Field was rapid. To handle the field's production, a six-mile pipeline was constructed to the railroad at Jennings, where a 37,500-barrel storage tank was erected. Later, a refinery, the first in Louisiana, was constructed at Jennings to handle the field's output. Other pipelines were constructed to Lake Charles, Butte La

Rose, and the Atchafalaya River to move the flow of crude, but storage and shipping facilities could not keep up with production, which was soon in excess of 80,000 barrels per day. Nearly every well drilled was a gusher producing between 2,500 and 10,000 barrels daily; once it was estimated that nearly 7,000,000 barrels of crude were being stored in the pool's earthen tanks.

As new gushers were brought in with astonishing rapidity, land values soared. Leases near known producers were sold for as high as ten thousand dollars an acre. The town of Jennings boomed. From a quiet rice-market town, Jennings was transformed into a bustling oil boom town with speculators, lease hounds, and wildcatters scrambling for the best leases.

During the summer of 1904 the Producers Oil Company completed a gusher on the Latreille tract on the east side of the field. A seventy-thousand-barrel-per-day producer, it was the pool's largest single gusher. Another well, the Bass-Benckenstein, later was completed and yielded 1.5 million barrels of crude between September 8, 1904, and January 31, 1905.

The Producers Oil Company was a subsidiary of the Texas Company (later Texaco), which was to play a big role in the development of the Louisiana petroleum industry. That corporation's initial involvement in the state began in September, 1902, when it began marketing, production, and refining operations in Louisiana. It soon became active in the Vinton, Naborton, Elm Grove, and Homer pools.

During the final half of 1905, more than 6,000,000 barrels of petroleum were produced by Jennings's wells. Production continued to climb until the field peaked in 1906 with an output of 9,025,000 barrels. In 1909 the Jennings Field produced 1,966,614 barrels of crude, valued at $1,421,806 at the then-current price of $0.723 per barrel. The following year the value of the field's output was pegged at $1,187,312. Afterward, annual production dropped drastically, falling to below 1,000,000 barrels in 1913.

For a while the Heywood Company used a huge air compressor plant, with more than twenty massive compressors powered by about fifty steam boilers, to stimulate production. However, saltwater began to intrude, and wells would produce thousands of barrels of saltwater every day for a few hundred barrels of oil. The field's output continued to decline until 1929, when the Yount Lee Oil Company located a deep stratum of oil near the 7,300-foot level. With this discovery the output of the Jennings Pool again began to climb. In 1939 a high point of 8,118,000 barrels of crude was produced. Afterward, production again began to decline, but at a much slower rate than before.

Owners of the Heywood Brothers Oil Corporation and drillers of the discovery well at Jennings (as numbered in the photograph beginning at the top left): (1) Alba Heywood, (2) Dewey Heywood, (3) O. W. Heywood, and (4) W. Scott Heywood, who was drilling superintendent of the firm. *Jennings Carnegie Public Library.*

A view of the Jennings No. 1 filling an earthen storage pit. The information written on the photograph in later years is in error about the completion date, the assertion that it was the first well in which screen was used to prevent sanding, and the depth at which production was encountered. This information is actually correct for the Jennings Oil Company No. 2. *Ron Shultz.*

The men who drilled the discovery well at Jennings that gave birth to the Louisiana petroleum industry. *Left to right*: Doug Phelps, C. O. Noble, Elmer Dobbins, Sank Hendricks, and W. Scott Heywood. *Ron Shultz*.

Left: The Jennings Oil Company No. 2 burning in 1902. This was the first well to use screen successfully to prevent sand from plugging the pipe. The success of this well spurred the continued development of the Jennings Field. *Jennings Carnegie Public Library. Right*: The Southern Oil Company's No. 3 well gushing high above its derrick at Jennings. A crowd has gathered to gaze at the spectacular sight. Note a roughneck viewing the scene from high on the derrick to the left. *Jennings Carnegie Public Library*.

Another fire at Jennings; perhaps another view of the Jennings Oil Company No. 2. Fires were common here as at other early oil fields. The technology of the period had not caught up with the massive production possible at the turn of the century with the discovery of new fields such as Jennings. Thus, inadequate technology and inexperience combined to create frequent accidents, explosions, and fires. *Ron Shultz.*

Oil flowing under gas pressure from a newly completed well fills an earthen storage pit at Jennings. Another pit in the foreground is ready to be filled. *Jennings Carnegie Public Library.*

The tremendous outpouring of crude at Jennings necessitated the construction of earthen storage lakes. Here, men with teams of mules and slips are digging such a storage facility. Unlike oil-producing areas in northern Louisiana and southern Arkansas, where ravines and valleys could be dammed to produce storage lakes, the terrain in southern Louisiana is flat, and the lakes had to be scraped out. *Ron Shultz.*

Left: Another fire at Jennings. This is an oil pit burning out of control. *Ron Shultz. Right*: Massive fires like this one were frequent occurrences at Jennings. Here, two men in the foreground casually lean against a fence to watch the inferno. *Jennings Carnegie Public Library.*

A crew of fire fighters battles a blaze at Jennings. A blast of steam from a boiler is being pumped onto the fire from the left. The men in the middle also seem to be preparing to spray the flames. Such work obviously was hot and dangerous. *Jennings Carnegie Public Library.*

W. Scott Heywood, one of the pioneers of the Jennings Field, in later years. Heywood remained in the oil business in Jennings throughout his life. *Ron Shultz.*

A crew of rig builders at work for the Mathison Oil Company at Evangeline in February, 1907. The town of Evangeline, just northeast of Jennings, was located near many of the producing wells of the pool, and the field often is referred to as the Evangeline Field. Note the closeness of the derricks in the background. *Mark Stewart and Eugene Spruell.*

A section of the oil field at Jennings shows a battery of small wooden storage tanks and the close spacing of the wells. *Jenning Carnegie Public Library.*

Another view of the Jennings Field. Note the extremely close spacing of the wells and the elevated pipeline in the foreground. *Ron Shultz.*

This forest of derricks demonstrates the density of wells at Jennings. *Jennings Carnegie Public Library.*

Another section of the Jennings Field, with a fire in the background. As of 1982, only one of these original derricks remains standing, but many of the old wells are being offset by new ones. *Ron Shultz.*

The Jennings offices of the Royal Petroleum Company, operators of the first refinery in Louisiana. *Jennings Carnegie Public Library.*

The Royal Petroleum Company refinery, first refinery in Louisiana, at Jennings in 1903. *Jennings Carnegie Public Library.*

The office and employees of the Union Iron Works, an oil-field shop in the Jennings Field in 1906. *Jennings Carnegie Public Library.*

Left: Another producer at Jennings. Crude is being blown out of the hose high up on the derrick. *Ron Shultz*. *Right*: Black roustabouts, like these men at Jennings, were a relatively rare sight in the early oil fields. The man on the left apparently was working barefooted. *Zigler Museum, Jennings, Louisiana*.

Louisiana's many waterways often were the first means of transporting crude oil to market once a new field had been found. At Jennings the Heywood brothers constructed a barge-loading facility on Bayou Nezpique on the Mermentau River to handle the output of the Jennings Field. *PennWell Publishing Company*.

Jennings was the scene of many gushers like this one. Production from such wells quickly outstripped the ability of small storage tanks, like the ones in this scene, to store the crude. *Ron Shultz.*

The Jaenke Bridge on the main road to the oil fields near Jennings. *Zigler Museum, Jennings, Louisiana.*

A gas well burns out of control near Trees, Louisiana, on May 25, 1913. *Jack Norman.*

Caddo

THE first natural gas deposits in northwestern Louisiana were discovered near Shreveport in 1870. At that time the Shreveport Ice Manufacturing Co. began work on a water well on the south bank of Cross Bayou, where present-day Market Street crossed the bayou. The well had reached 961 feet when the workers quit for the day. After dark, a night watchman making his rounds became curious and began to inspect the drilling equipment. Noticing a strange wind coming from the well, he struck a match to see better. The area instantly exploded into flames, and the watchman fled in terror. Later, the fire was extinguished, and for several years the gas escaping from the well was used to light homes and businesses in the area.

In 1902, Ellison M. Adger of Belcher, Louisiana, began a water well near Dixie (on Cottonwood Bayou in the Soda Lake region). Adger's goal was to locate sufficient water for his livestock, but at 425 feet all he had found was saltwater, and he abandoned the hole. Unwilling to quit his search for water, Adger decided to send soil samples to A. C. Veatch (or Vetch) of the U.S. Geological Survey, asking if they indicated whether he would be able to strike an artesian well in the region. Veatch, who had examined the region around Caddo (or Ferry) Lake, replied that he believed there was no water in the area, but that if a well were sunk to the one-thousand-foot level, the driller would probably strike oil or natural gas. Adger, not interested in oil or gas, promptly gave up his search, commenting that Veatch's prediction "sounded like a fairy tale."

The prospect of petroleum had brought other men to the region, however, and in 1904 an oil well drilled by Savage and Morrical penetrated the predicted oil-bearing formation. When the well did not flow, the hole was abandoned. The next year the Latex Oil and Pipe Line Company located two producing horizons in the area, but the gas flow was so strong that the hole was plugged.

Oil men, now certain that oil could be found in the Caddo Lake area, soon had several wells underway. In 1905 the Latex Oil and Pipe Line Company sank a well into two producing sands, but a strong flow of natural gas again caused them to abandon the hole. The region's high gas pressure would continue to plague their efforts. In May, 1905, the Producers No. 2 was abandoned after it struck a pocket of natural gas that blew the well out. Improper sealing of the well allowed gas to flow around the casing in the hole, and the escaping gas quickly tore away the surface formations and cratered the hole. Somehow the escaping gas caught fire, and the derrick and machinery sank into the fiery crater. A short time later, the Producers No. 3 was completed, but once more the pressure of the underground pocket of natural gas was too great. Other drillers likewise were plagued by the problem; one well, the Caddo Oil and Gas Company's No. 1, blew in wild and continued to spew natural gas into the air for three years before it could be controlled.

Although this strong gas flow greatly hindered drillers, it indicated to oil men that a large deposit of crude was nearby, and the Caddo Lake area was soon extensively leased. As the search continued, the Savage brothers completed Caddo's first oil well, the No. 1 Auffenhauser, on March 28, 1906. At first the heavy gas flow delayed further development of the field, but eventually those with optimism were rewarded. In 1907 a group of citizens from nearby Dixie and Belcher, located on the Red River to the east of Caddo Lake, organized the Dixie Oil, Gas, and Pipe Line Company and imported a driller from Corsicana, Texas. The site selected for their first well was near the spot where Adger had struck saltwater five years earlier. At 825 feet the bit penetrated a pocket of gas that flowed an estimated one million cubic feet per day. But it was oil that the investors wanted, and the drilling continued. At 2,167 feet an oil sand was found, but the crude was not in producing quantity, and the hole was abandoned.

Undaunted, the driller moved his rig about a mile and began a new hole. Once again a strong flow of natural gas was struck, and the well ran wild for several weeks before it was capped. Later this well supplied natural gas to Dixie, Uni, and Belcher. By 1909, eleven natural gas wells had been drilled in the vicinity of Caddo. That same year a six-inch pipeline was laid from Dixie to Shreveport so the latter community could also be supplied with gas. Eventually this pipeline network was expanded to include Mooringsport, Blanchard, and Caddo, and it was estimated that twenty-seven hundred domestic customers and twenty-eight industrial firms were using Caddo Lake gas.

Despite some commercial use, much of the natural gas was wasted. After the Ananaias Hunting and Fishing Club No. 1 well blew in wild in 1906, the Louisiana legislature enacted a law that permitted the state's Engineering Department to take control of wild wells and enabled the state to appropriate enough adjoining land, after warning the owners, to cover the expense of capping the runaway. However, the law made no mention of a method of enforcement, and it was not effective.

Most oil men believed that if they could somehow get rid of the natural gas in the Caddo area, oil could be found in profitable quantities. By 1906 the area, despite the problem, was producing 4,560 barrels of crude annually, and knowledgeable observers realized its production could be increased if the natural gas could be vented off. Month after month, millions of cubic feet of natural gas were allowed to escape into the atmosphere. So great was the roar of escaping gas that it could be heard several miles away by residents of the town of Caddo. The gas came from the earth in such huge quantities that a reported twenty-five miles of the countryside was lit by burning gas. In 1907 some seventy million cubic feet of natural gas were wasted daily.

As a result of the rush to get rid of the natural gas, there were several large oil-well fires. One well near Oil City, on the northeast shore of Caddo Lake, burned out of control for five years before it was extinguished. The crater was ninety feet deep and three hundred feet wide, and it was estimated that twenty-five million cubic feet of natural gas a day were consumed by the flames. It and several other nearby burning wells lit up the area around the lake brilliantly at night. Finally in 1908 the Louisiana General Assembly made it a criminal offense to allow a gas well to blow out of control or burn or to allow natural gas to escape into the atmosphere.

The tremendous natural gas pressure was not the only problem associated with drilling in the Caddo Lake area. The land was swampy and generally covered with overflow water. Drillers had to cut huge cypress timbers to construct a boxlike structure reaching above the high water mark as a safe foundation for their derrick. During the wet season it was difficult for mules and wagons to negotiate the swampy area, and oxen were used to haul in heavy material loaded onto skids.

In 1907 the producing area was extended across Caddo Lake when J. B. McCann, an employee of the J. M. Guffey Petroleum Company, traced the flow of escaping natural gas across the water by boat. Often the volume of escaping gas was so great that McCann could ignite the vapor and simply follow the flames across the water to the opposite shore. Once he had traced the gas to its source, McCann leased nearly one thousand acres. He decided to sink the first well on the Hostetter farm, where, after only twelve days of drilling, the bit at 800 feet penetrated a pocket of fifteen million cubic feet of natural gas. Another well, the Hostetter No. 1, was sunk about one-quarter mile to the south, but it blew out of control at 2,208 feet and was abandoned. Named for its founder, who had first entered the oil business in 1872, the J. M. Guffey Petroleum Company was a predecessor of the Gulf Refining Company of Louisiana, a subsidiary of the Gulf Oil Corporation, which was chartered in Pennsylvania in 1922 and became a giant in the Louisiana petroleum industry.

In July, 1907, two other wells extended the proven area to the south and southwest of Caddo City. That year twenty-three wells were completed in the region. Eight produced oil, and eleven were gas wells. Oil production climbed to 44,908 barrels of crude annually, but the field's major production continued to be natural gas. An estimated seventy million cubic feet of natural gas a day were reportedly being wasted in the Caddo Field, and residents of Shreveport, twenty-five miles to the southeast, could see the flames from the burning gas.

Just as the year 1908 began, the Hostetter No. 4, drilled by the Caddo Gas and Oil Company, created one of the region's most unusual sights. A great effort had been made to keep the well from blowing in wild. However, the surface casing had been cemented in so firmly that the gas, which thereby was blocked from escaping through the well's hole, seeped through underground fissures and erupted half a mile away in the channel of Caddo Lake. Water was thrown twenty feet into the air by the escaping gas, and the spectacle did not end until the well was opened and the gas pressure eased. Eventually the Hostetter No. 4 was cemented all the way to the bottom of the casing before the flow was totally checked.

Oil men quickly recognized Caddo's unusual characteristics. When a well was completed, there would be a profitable flow of crude for the first few hours. Then, often without warning, there would be a tremendous eruption of natural gas, which would close off the oil flow and cause the well to run wild. The blowout would soon form a huge crater around the well head. Caddo, like all other oil fields, held oil, gas, and water trapped in underground layers of porous rock. Gas, the lightest of the three, rose to the top of the trap, where it was prevented from escaping by an impervious layer of dome-shaped rock. Consequently, the gas collected on the top and sides of the trap. Below the natural gas the rock pores were filled with petroleum, often with oil and gas mixed in a solution. Beneath the gas and oil, water accumulated at the bottom of the trap and held the gas and crude firmly against the impervious rock under great pressure. Usually when the drilling bit penetrated the rock dome, the oil and gas gushed to the surface, to the delight of the oil men. However, at Caddo the gas pressure was so strong that whenever the dome was penetrated, the first great rush would rupture the impervious rock trap and the softer rocks above it. As a result, much to the dismay of oil men, the entire structure caved in, often within hours and often dragging the drilling rig and equipment into the chasm.

On May 13, 1908, nature worked against oil men with disastrous effect. The Dawes Trustee No. 1 had been brought in two days earlier, and while the crew was running casing, the well blew in at 1,400 feet. The estimated gas production was forty million cubic feet, and the crew was frantically struggling to cap the runaway when a tornado struck and destroyed the derrick. Naturally this loss delayed the capping effort, which was further hampered when another gas horizon broke free and caught fire in June, burning freely until February 12, 1909.

Also in 1908, two prominent early-day Louisiana oil men, Mike Benedum and Joe Trees, arrived in the Caddo Lake Field. Recognizing that there obviously was a vast amount of crude at Caddo if a way could be devised to ease the huge gas pressure, Trees's father suggested that the oil men fill the drill hole with cement, allow it to harden, and then complete the well by drilling through the artificially created stable formation. Realizing that this might be the key to unlocking Caddo's riches, the two men quickly leased 130,000 acres in the vicinity and sank several shallow wells. The holes were pushed to just a few feet above the known oil- and gas-bearing formations and then were filled with cement—among the first such efforts in the nation. Once the cement hardened, the holes were completed into the oil and gas zone.

Benedum's and Trees's early efforts were unrewarded. Thus far the two men had spent approximately one hundred thousand dollars to develop their Caddo holdings but had recouped little return. They then decided that the key to Caddo was to drill deeper. Their next well was sunk six feet deeper than any previous well in the pool. Both men were standing on the derrick floor when the well blew in. Trees was smoking a cigar when gas roared out of the drill hole. Terrified of sparking an inferno, he hurriedly extinguished his smoke. With the gas came oil, one hundred barrels an hour at first. Eventually, the well stabilized at three thousand barrels a day.

Benedum and Trees had solved the puzzle of tapping Caddo's riches, but they had created another problem for themselves. Although the two oil men had acquired extensive leases throughout the Caddo area, their property included only dry landholdings, while much of the field was covered with lakes and bayous. Because Benedum and Trees held most of the dry-land leases, Gulf Oil Company and several other producers in the Caddo region acquired adjoining leases in the water surrounding Benedum's and Trees's holdings, much to the dismay of the partners.

However, offset production by rival companies was not Benedum's and Trees's greatest concern. Within a short time the two oil men had nearly eight hundred thousand barrels of oil in storage from their Caddo wells. Standard Oil offered them $0.39 a barrel for their crude but sold its own production for $1.40 per barrel. At first Benedum and Trees searched for other markets; crude was marketed to area cotton mills for $0.70 per barrel, and a pipeline was built to a rail outlet to ship the oil to more distant markets. But just as it appeared that the two oil men were on the verge of opening the bottleneck, the railroad informed them that no more tank cars were available. After discovering that one of Standard's officers also was a director of the railroad, Benedum complained to federal officials. Afterward the railroad recounted its tank cars, discovered some that had been overlooked, and resumed shipments.

To insure that they would be freed of dependence on Standard Oil for marketing their Caddo production, Benedum and Trees announced plans to build their own refinery in Caddo. Land was purchased, plans drawn, and outlets developed. Recognizing that such a facility would greatly reduce its own profit, the Ohio Oil Company, a subsidiary of Standard, offered Benedum and Trees five million dollars in cash, with another one million dollars to come after Standard Oil had produced five million dollars' worth of Caddo crude. Benedum and Trees accepted the offer.

Standard and its subsidiaries continued to develop the Caddo Field during the following years, and the pool was an extremely profitable addition to Standard's holdings. The production from one well in the pool repaid Standard for half of the entire amount paid to Benedum and Trees. It was estimated that Benedum's and Trees's leases eventually produced one billion dollars' worth of oil and natural gas.

These were not the only oil companies closely tied to the Caddo Lake Field. The Purified Petroleum Products Company of Louisiana, Limited, based in Shreveport, having patented a process of treating gasoline and kerosene by a combination of heat and mechanical equipment, built a facility, connected to the Caddo discovery by a four-inch pipeline, on twenty-one acres at Gas Center, Louisiana. The company continued to operate in this way until October, 1913, when the Louisiana Oil Refining Company was organized to acquire Purified's property. A majority of stock also was acquired in the Louisiana Oil Exporting Company, which owned shipping facilities at Chalmette on the Mississippi River near New Orleans. In April, 1917, another expansion took place in which the Louisiana Oil Exporting Company, the Southern Oil Company, Lewis Drilling Company, Amateur Oil Company, Caddo Drilling Company, Arkla Oil Company, Verbena Oil Company, and Union Gas and Pipe Line Company were merged with the Louisiana Oil Refining Company to form the Louisiana Oil Refining Corporation. From that time on, the company became one of the major producers in the state.

The tremendous waste that resulted from the activity at Caddo prompted a visit to the field by David T. Day and C. W. Hayes of the United States Geological Survey. After viewing the burning Trustee No. 1, these appalled officials persuaded federal officials to intervene in the state's oil fields. Reporting to President Theodore Roosevelt, they charged that the wasted natural gas from the Caddo Field equaled one-twentieth of the total gas consumption of the entire country. When federal officials discovered that some land in the Caddo Field was still in the public domain, Roosevelt ordered the secretary of the interior in 1908 to ban entry to, appropriation of, and withdrawal from settlement of all public land in nearly sixty-five hundred acres of oil-producing land, effectively denying it to exploration by oil men. State legislators also in 1908 enacted Act 268 which permitted the Board of Commissioners of the Caddo Levee District to lease lands for oil and gas.

Later, in 1910, President William H. Taft established the Petroleum Reserve No. 4, which contained about 414,720 acres in the Caddo region. On some plots oil men had already begun drilling, and when the land was closed, several lawsuits resulted. Not until 1923 were the last of these cases settled in the United States Supreme Court.

Other laws were passed annulling several applications on file at the state Land Office for drilling rights at Caddo, and Louisiana's first conservation law, enacted in 1906, making it unlawful to permit a well to "go wild" or "burn wastefully," was the beginning of state control of the Louisiana petroleum industry. Two years later, in 1908, a Commission of Natural Resources was organized; in 1910 it was changed to the Department of Mining and Minerals, and two years later, in 1912, to the Department of Conservation. Once the enforcement mechanism was established, a series of legislative acts followed to regulate oil, natural gas, and pipelines.

During the controversy over the tremendous waste of natural gas in the Caddo area, production in the field, near the end of 1909, was pushed to a new and deeper horizon. On the west side on James (or Jeems) Bayou, near the western edge of the Caddo Field, the J. C. Trees No. 4 was brought in as a two-thousand-barrel-per-day producer from below 2,300 feet. Within a month the well's daily flow had increased to three thousand barrels, and several other "deep" well were underway in the area. In April, 1910, the Gulf Refining Company's No. 1 Burr was brought in at a depth of 2,225 feet with an output of two thousand barrels daily. However, the big bonanza occurred in late June that year when the Producers Oil Company completed its Producers No. 6 well, from which flowed twelve thousand barrels of oil every twenty-four hours.

By 1910 most of the land around Caddo Lake had been leased, but approximately eight thousand acres of the lake bottom itself were still unclaimed. The extensive production around the lake had convinced most oil men that the lake bottom would yield huge amounts of oil and natural gas but that a huge outlay of capital would be required to tap the wealth. In 1910 the Caddo Levee Board decided to lease the bed of Caddo Lake to oil men piecemeal. For seventeen years Caddo Lake had remained relatively low. Each year following spring rains the water level would rise to what was called the "raft level," but then it would quickly fall. Oil men hoped that eventually the lake would completely dry up and allow them easy access to the oil beneath its bottom. However, the federal government announced in 1910 that it was going to dam the lake in 1911 and raise the water to its original level. This news forced the Levee Board to alter its plans.

There had been some previous attempts in California at offshore drilling by building piers from the land over the water and then drilling from the piers. However, that technique was impractical to adapt to Caddo Lake; some of the well sites would be a mile from the nearest shore and at least one-eighth of a mile apart. To connect them with piers would mean criss-crossing the lake, which would close it to navigation. As a result, only the Gulf Refining Company of Louisiana submitted a last-minute bid to acquire the lease.

Gulf proposed to drill a minimum of five wells and to pay a cash bonus of thirty thousand dollars and a one-eighth royalty on the first two hundred barrels of oil per well and one-sixteenth on the remainder of the production. After a total production of three hundred thousand barrels was reached, Gulf would pay an additional seventy thousand dollars. The first wells were staked along the north shore of the lake, and within a short time W. B. Pyron, Gulf's production superintendent for Louisiana; Frank Chalk, his assistant; and Henry Melat, the drilling superintendent, began work.

Melat planned to construct permanent drilling platforms on the lake, with one platform every six hundred feet on each ten-acre site. Once a site was staked, 140 cypress logs would be cut and barged to the location. Driven into the lake bottom, they would be used to support the drilling platform and a separate boiler setting. The boiler setting was to be about one hundred feet from the drilling platform to reduce the potential for fire, and the two units would be connected by a walkway. Melat gathered a fleet of three tugboats, ten barges, a floating pile driver, and several smaller vessels, and within a short time work was well underway. Pre-cut lumber was used to build the platforms, and once construction was completed, the actual drilling began. The barges hauled rigs to the platforms constructed. After erecting the derricks, the drillers attached a series of fifty-gallon barrels to additional posts to serve as the wells' slush pits. In May, 1911, the world's first offshore well—the Ferry Lake No. 1—was completed.

Once a well was completed, the boiler and steam engine were removed. Pumping was handled by a twenty-five-horsepower gasoline engine requiring two large flywheels; it was housed thirty to forty feet from the well to minimize the possibility of a fire. The pump was connected to the engine by a long belt. Unfortunately, despite these precautions fires were common. Often the lake was swept by windstorms that threw spray on the power belt. The wet belt would slip, and if a well's crew was unable to cut off the gasoline engine fast enough, the resulting friction often would ignite the belt and then the entire well.

Within a short time the Gulf Refining Company was bringing in gusher after gusher from beneath the lake's surface. Despite this increased oil production, the Caddo Field's gas pressure did not drop significantly. In fact, in 1911 this gas pressure caused the field's greatest disaster. On May 12 that year the Producers Oil Company's Harrell No. 7, a well on dry land, was completed with an estimated flush production of forty thousand barrels. As with all other wells in the region, the gas pressure in the No. 7 Harrell was tremendous, and as the crew was making the final connections, the well blew out. The heat generated by sand blowing up the pipe ignited the escaping gas, and four men were badly burned, one of them fatally, in the initial fire.

Flames roared seventy-five feet into the air as nearby oil companies rushed men and equipment to extinguish the blaze. All trees for a distance of fifty yards from the No. 7 Harrell were removed to keep the flames from spreading, and three batteries of six boilers each poured steam and water on the burning well without result. An attempt then was made to put out the fire by shooting the burning well with a cannon, but twelve-pound cannonballs proved insufficient to break the blazing stream of oil and gas. Eventually forty men working in two shifts dug a fifty-foot tunnel fifteen feet below the surface to the well. The task took a week to complete, but when it was finished the tunnel allowed the broken casing to be diverted into the tunnel, and the fire was extinguished. The monetary loss eventually was pegged at $175,000.

While such spectacular disasters attracted the public's attention, the region's oil production continued to mount, as the Caddo Lake oil and gas pool was developed more rapidly than any other within the state. Production in 1908 amounted to 499,937 barrels of crude from fifty-six wells. The following year, 183 wells produced a total of 1,028,818 barrels, and by 1910 Caddo's production had reached 5,090,793 barrels.

Such an upsurge in production proved a boon to local residents as royalty and bonus payments by oil companies increased along with the flow of crude. One storekeeper at Mooringsport, on the southeast shore of Caddo Lake, received as much as thirty thousand dollars per month in bonuses and royalties on land he originally had purchased for seventy-five cents an acre. When oil production doubled between 1908 and 1909, the price of leases in the Caddo Region jumped from fifty dollars an acre to one thousand dollars. So great had Caddo's production become that, shortly after Patrick C. Boyle established the *Oil and Gas Journal* in 1910, the publication opened a branch office at Shreveport.

Eventually several smaller fields were incorporated into the greater Caddo Pool.

The Ferry Lake district was opened to production in 1915, and the Mooringsport, Oil City, James Bayou, Monterey, Harts Ferry, Vivian, Black Bayou, and Pine Island fields had been uncovered by 1917. Other nearby production was found in the DeSoto and Red River districts, the Naborton Field, the Crichton Field, Gusher Bend, and the Grand Bayou district.

The year 1918 proved to be a high point in terms of the amount of crude pouring from the earth, with 11,144,000 barrels pumped. Afterward, production began a slow but steady decline. By 1939 the estimated total natural gas production of the Caddo Field was 136,525,867,000 cubic feet. In addition, between 1906 and 1942 the field produced 159,770,000 barrels of crude.

By touching off the oil rush in Louisiana, the Caddo Lake discovery also gave birth to several boom towns. Before the opening of the field, the nearby area was mostly marshy land covered with tall grass and crossed by bayous. The danger of being caught in the muck was ever-present; quicksand was sometimes encountered. In addition, thick stands of cypress covered with moss dotted the region. There were no roads and only a few trails. In fact, most travelers in the area still needed a compass. Stories abounded of men and teams of mules suddenly swallowed up by the soft earth.

After the discovery, however, the area was flooded with lease hounds, speculators, promoters, and oil-field workers. Overnight, Oil City, Vivian, and Mooringsport became bustling boom towns filled with oil men. Saloons, gambling dens, and brothels were everywhere, and leases were bought and sold "in a wild frenzy." Men flocked to the area to brave the humid weather, mosquitoes, ticks, and poor drinking water, to sleep in tents or shacks, and to earn $2.50 a day for a twelve-hour shift in the oil fields.

Mike Benedum and Joe Trees, who had done so much to open the field and who controlled a large portion of the leased area, formed the Trees Oil Company, with headquarters at the Youree Hotel in Shreveport, to handle their Louisiana investments. The Kansas City Southern Railroad had a stop at Lewis, near Caddo Lake, and the partners often would leave Shreveport at 8:00 A.M. by train, ride to Lewis, inspect their operations, and then catch the 5:00 or 6:00 P.M. train back to Shreveport.

Lewis quickly became the center for those working in the field. However, conditions there were bad at best. The men bunked where they could find space—in neighborhood farmhouses, tents, shacks, barns, or anyplace that offered cover from the elements. Both food and water were in short supply, and the men were expected to shift for themselves. Corduroy roads, built across the swamps to the drilling sites, had to be rebuilt almost as quickly as they were completed because logs and timbers sank out of sight under the traffic. Close on the heels of the workers came camp followers, whose main concern was to separate oil men from their wages. Overnight, tents and shacks appeared near the wells, and in them were offered gambling, liquor, and women. The workers were lonely and bored, and they often spent their week's wages in a one-night binge in "town." Law enforcement officials lacked the men to control the huge influx of "thieves, thugs, outlaws, and rowdies that swarmed into the area." Robbery, assault, and homicide became daily events, while fistfights drew little if any attention.

To bring order to the situation, Benedum and Trees hired a deputy sheriff, a former Texas Ranger, during his off-duty hours and placed him on the Trees Oil Company payroll. This worked for a while, but one man could not maintain the peace. A climax was reached when a crew of blacks was hired to build storage tanks for a recently completed well. The well crew was "undependable, hot-tempered and arrogant" and refused to work with the blacks. Faced with this situation, Benedum and Trees built a wire fence around the well, brought the deputy sheriff to the scene, and put the tank crew to work anyway. Seven or eight of the drilling crew, mounted on horses, suddenly appeared and demanded that the blacks stop work. They were confronted by the deputy sheriff, who told the men that he was there to keep the peace. Shouts and curses began to be leveled at the blacks, and five or six of the drilling crew dismounted and started through the wire fence. The deputy thereupon drew his gun and opened fire. Several of the drilling crew were wounded, and the rest fled. The wounded were loaded aboard a special train and taken to the nearest hospital, where they recovered. Later they were tried, convicted, and sentenced to the road gang.

Although the small riot had been stopped, Benedum and Trees had had enough. They decided to build their own town to protect their workers against outsiders. Selecting a cotton patch about four or five miles from Lewis and near the Texas-Louisiana state line, just north of Caddo Lake and near one of their leases, the partners began building a camp. Frame houses were erected for workers, and machine shops and other facilities were constructed to service their leases. Eventually a regular community was established. Several other buildings, including stores, hotels, churches, a doctor's office, a pool hall, a dance pavilion, a post office, and a company office were built. No saloons or gambling dens were allowed. Named Trees, the community was "the first of its kind built by an oil company strictly for employees."

The Savage brothers' No. 1 Auffenhauser, first oil well in the great Caddo Field (1906). *Estate of M. Carl Jones.*

On the derrick floor of a rotary rig in the Caddo Field. The well is the Chew fee No. 1, and the crew is from the drilling firm of Bill Spain (fourth from the left). Note the exposed chain drives used to transfer power from steam engines to the gears that drove the rotary to the left of center in the photograph. Working in the proximity of such exposed chain drives was dangerous, and workers had to remain alert and careful. *Jack Norman.*

Oil and gas fires were common in the Caddo Field. This huge oil fire, the Star Oil Company's Loucke No. 3, burned out of control near Mooringsport with an estimated daily loss of thirty thousand barrels. It was considered to be the largest single oil-well fire in the United States to that time. *Louisiana State University at Shreveport Archives.*

Wild gas wells were commonplace in the Caddo area. As in other parts of Louisiana and southern Arkansas, wells frequently cratered, swallowing up entire drilling rigs. Here, a tremendous gas geyser is in action near Oil City, Louisiana. The photograph was taken on August 25, 1912, when the well was losing one hundred million cubic feet of natural gas per day. *Louisiana State Library*.

A view of James Bayou, just off Caddo Lake. Note the cypress trees and the platform walkway constructed to the derricks in the background. *Jack Norman*.

Oil wells on James Bayou near Stacey's Landing in the Caddo Field. *Louisiana State University at Shreveport Archives.*

The first significant offshore drilling in the United States took place in the waters of Caddo Lake. The rig in the foreground is the Ferry Lake No. 1, the first of many such wells to be completed on the lake. In this photograph, crews are laying pipeline to the well. *Jack Norman.*

A view of the Ferry Lake No. 1. The derrick was built on pilings driven into the lake bottom. A small catwalk was extended from the shore to the well. *Graydon F. Smart*, Shreveport Magazine.

Caddo Lake oil wells in 1907. *Mark Stewart and Eugene Spruell.*

By 1919, Caddo Lake was thickly covered with offshore wells. *Louisiana State Library.*

Left: One of the most spectacular oil-well fires in the Caddo Field was the Producer's Oil Company's Harrell No. 7. The well caught fire on May 12, 1911. Note the pipe on the left that has been taken from the flame, twisted by the heat. Two men died when the well ignited, and several others were burned. *Louisiana State University at Shreveport Archives. Right*: The Harrell No. 7 burned ferociously from May 12 to June 6, 1911. The oil men resorted to several measures to combat the fire, including shields of corrugated sheet metal to protect themselves from the heat. A photographer in the left foreground prepares his camera, mounted on a tripod, to record the dramatic event. *Louisiana State University at Shreveport Archives.*

This cannon, firing a twelve-pound ball, was used in an attempt to fight the Harrell No. 7 blaze. Driller M. Carl Jones recalled that an attempt was made to shoot the valve off the well, as it was stuck partially open, causing the flames from the burning gas to be spewed broadly instead of shooting straight up in a relatively small column. If the stuck valve could have been removed, the fire could have been fought much more easily. Unfortunately, as Jones recalled, the men manning the cannon were poor marksmen, and they never managed to hit the valve. *Jack Norman.*

Dated May 19, 1911, this photograph depicts the third attempt to put out the fire at the Harrell No. 7. The men used sheet-metal shields to get close to the fire so they could attempt to extinguish it with high-pressure steam hoses fed by boilers. The photographer observed that the men were "working in the very jaws of death." *Estate of M. Carl Jones.*

Left: The Harrell No. 7 was eventually extinguished by means of a pipeline, laid through a tunnel, tapped into the well casing underground. *Jack Norman. Right*: In this photograph the pipeline is in place in the tunnel of the Harrell No. 7, and the men are preparing to connect it to the well. This final attempt to put out the fire was successful. *W. B. Grabill.*

A drilling crew on a rotary rig near Oil City in 1907. The man on the far left is Jack Angel. Alex Rice, the driller, is seated. *Estate of M. Carl Jones.*

A cable-tool drilling rig and crew at Vivian, Louisiana. The top of the massive drill bit is shown at the bottom of the photograph, hanging at the end of the cable. Cable-tool rigs functioned essentially by raising and dropping the heavy drill bit, allowing it to pound its way into the earth. The power to raise the heavy bit frequently was provided by a steam engine supplied by a boiler. Note the huge bull wheel around which the cable for raising and lowering the bit was wound. The men in the photograph are wearing knee-high boots, a popular and often necessary form of footwear for slogging through the muddy oil fields. Note the restaurant in the far left background of the photograph. *Jack Norman.*

Oil storage tanks were another source of fires in the Caddo Oil Field. This 55,000-barrel steel storage tank was struck by lightning on August 10, 1912. Such fires were virtually impossible to extinguish and generally had to burn themselves out. *Estate of M. Carl Jones.*

The boom town of Oil City, Louisiana, on October 15, 1912. For a time, drunks and other offenders were chained to the tree remaining in the middle of the street. *Jack Norman.*

Unloading pipe for the oil fields onto wagons from railroad cars at Vivian, Louisiana. Wagons with mule and sometimes ox teams were required to get the heavy loads to the oil fields, because the primitive roads were broken down by the constant hauling of heavy equipment and supplies. The intense traffic, coupled with the usual rainfall in the area, quickly caused the road systems to turn to muck. *Jack Norman.*

This Standard Oil Company well at Vivian, brought in on March 20, 1911, has drawn an interested crowd of onlookers. *Louisiana State Library.*

The main street of Vivian in 1909. This photograph shows a wide range of conveyances: a boy on a bicycle, several automobiles, a man on horseback, and a number of horse-drawn buckboards and wagons. *Jack Norman.*

The movie theater at Vivian was host for a show from the famous Miller Brothers' 101 Ranch in Oklahoma. The production was brought to the theater by a vehicle from the ranch. Note the bull horns on the radiator cap of the bus and the saddle on display in front of the theater. *Jack Norman.*

The Moonshine Pharmacy at Vivian featured cold drinks, cigars, and prescriptions. The two vehicles belonging to "The Hustler" were probably a taxi service for getting oil men and lease hounds to the fields. *Jack Norman.*

The interior of the McKeever and Hammock Blacksmith Shop at Vivian. Such shops were important for keeping in action the many mules and horses used to haul equipment, supplies, and workers to the oil fields. Many blacksmith shops also served to repair oil-field equipment until more specialized machine shops were established. *Jack Norman.*

The interior of Pop Haley's Restaurant at Vivian, probably in the 1920s. *Jack Norman.*

A Standard Oil Company of Louisiana service station at Vivian about 1920. Note the grease rack in the far lower right of the picture. Cars were simply driven up on this ramp so the mechanic could change the oil and lubricate the vehicle. *Jack Norman.*

A group of young ladies playing croquet at Vivian. Though living in a boom town had its difficulties, the general prosperity brought by oil benefited many. *Jack Norman.*

Another sign of prosperity: Main Street of the town of Vivian as it was being prepared for paving about 1918. *Jack Norman.*

Mooringsport, a boom town in the Caddo Field, in May, 1913. Derricks are scattered throughout the community. Caddo Lake can be seen in the upper left. *Jack Norman.*

A view of the east side of Mooringsport. Many wells were drilled within the city limits. *Jack Norman.*

This scene in the new boom town of Lewis, Louisiana, located along the tracks of the Texas and Pacific Railroad north of Shreveport, shows some of the very first buildings constructed in that community. *Jack Norman.*

Loading oil into railroad tank cars at Lewis. *Estate of M. Carl Jones.*

A panorama of the Pine Island Field. The pipes on the ground at right conveyed production from the wells to storage tanks. *Graydon F. Smart*, Shreveport Magazine.

Left: A deep sand well blowing wild on the R. K. Smith Lease at Pine Island in the 1920s. *Louisiana State University at Shreveport Archives*. *Right*: By 1925, steel derricks were in use at Pine Island. Here, two men construct a new steel derrick in that field. *Jack Norman*.

A forest of derricks rose around the shores of Clear Lake, part of the Pine Island Field, in the late 1920s. *Jack Norman.*

A ten-mule team belonging to the Ober Teaming Company hauls a boiler in the Pine Island Field in 1927. The boiler is being carried on an eight-wheel "walker" wagon. When the roads were especially muddy, the teamsters usually resorted to a twenty-mule or ox team. *Graydon F. Smart*, Shreveport Magazine.

East Texas Street at Edwards in Shreveport, Louisiana, in 1922. Shreveport was benefited tremendously by the oil fields in northwestern Louisiana, becoming the principal headquarters city for a number of oil companies. *W. B. Grabill.*

M. Carl Jones (*right*) with other oil men in his office in Shreveport. Jones was an outstanding drilling contractor who brought in many wells in northern Louisiana, southern Arkansas, and East Texas. *Estate of M. Carl Jones.*

Shreveport was the scene of some creative marketing of petroleum products. Here is Jerry's Service Station No. 2 as it appeared in 1930. *PennWell Publishing Company.*

Citizens of Shreveport witnessed an unusual scene in 1921 when the Red River changed its course and enveloped a wild gas well, presenting an unusually difficult problem in killing the well. Here, two barges have been anchored alongside the well. Note the spray dashing through a hole in the "derrick floor." The heavy barges were pitched about like corks by the escaping gas. *Mark Stewart and Eugene*

Trees City, Louisiana, one of the first oil company towns in the United States. The town, said by oil man Joe Trees to have been named after his wife, was built by Trees and his partner, Mike Benedum, to provide employees of their firm a positive alternative to living in boom towns like Lewis and Oil City. Trees logically believed that if his men had comfortable sleeping quarters, decent food, and wholesome recreation, they would be much more efficient employees. *Jack Norman.*

Another view of Trees City. The building in the center is the office of the Benedum and Trees Oil Company. *Graydon F. Smart*, Shreveport Magazine.

A drilling crew in the Caddo Field. Note the gun in the hand of the man on the left. It was not uncommon for hijackers to rob oil-field workers at the well sites; thus, some of the men armed themselves for protection. Rough-hewn logs were used as the support foundation for the derrick. *Estate of M. Carl Jones.*

A portable pole rig being prepared to spud in a well in the Bossier Oil Field, a shallow pool near Shreveport. The rig, owned by the National Oil Company, was mounted on the front end of a steam tractor, which, with its huge rear wheels, could simply be driven to the well site. *W. B. Grabill.*

THE strike at Caddo Lake touched off the oil rush to northern Louisiana, which proved to be one of Louisiana's richest petroleum-producing areas. Eventually several important fields were uncovered in the region. Of these, perhaps the most spectacular was the De Soto–Red River Field, located in De Soto and Red River parishes approximately thirty miles southeast of Shreveport and forty-five miles slightly east and south of the Caddo Field.

Attention was first directed to the area in 1904 when Caddo boomed, but not until eight years later, in 1912, would the region's first gas well be opened near Naborton, in De Soto Parish, at a depth of eight hundred feet. Eventually the search for crude would center in the area just north of Naborton along the Louisiana Railway and Navigation Company's tracks in what was called the Sabine Uplift.

Encouraged by the location of natural gas in the Nacatoch sand, several oil men decided to probe the area in hopes of locating a deeper productive sand, corresponding to what had been found at Caddo. The hunt was spurred on by the location of several wells producing small quantities, and in the spring of 1913, G. C. Matson toured De Soto Parish and outlined the general structural features. About the same time, on May 10, 1913, the Gulf Refining Company successfully completed its Jenkins No. 2, thereby opening the Naborton District to production.

Within a short time of the Gulf Refining find, Naborton became a center of frenzied activity. The productive area was followed eastward into Red River Parish, and in April, 1914, the Marston No. 1 opened the Abington District to production. The Naborton District underwent its greatest development within twelve months of the discovery. However, oil men continued to follow production across the Red River into the Crichton District, which was opened in November, 1914. By 1915, the Crichton area was the scene of most of the drilling activity.

The De Soto–Red River Field is made up of many small regions containing numerous large wells surrounded by barren areas. Just to the south of Naborton is the Naborton Dome. Starting along the west edge of Bayou Pierre Lake and extending southward is the Smithport Anticline. South of the Naborton Dome is the Bice Anticline. Also in the area are the Crichton Terrace, the Gusher Bend Anticline, and the Gusher Bend Fault, and several minor faults run through the field. Another nearby producing area was found near Pelican, along the border of southern De Soto and northern Sabine parishes. Sixteen wells were drilled in the Pelican District, as the region became known, but only about ten were producers. Although a small pool of oil was found, inadequate production hindered continued development of the area.

Starting in 1913, the De Soto–Red River area was extensively developed despite the fact that the region had a high ratio of dry holes to producing wells. In fact, in 1915 the number of dusters was nearly equal to the number of producers. By 1914, total production for the De Soto–Red River Field amounted to only 4,236,251 barrels—3,834,593 from De Soto Parish, which included the output from the Pelican District, and 401,622 from Red River Parish. The next year, 1915, production figures reflect an eastward movement of drilling activity as the De Soto area's output dropped to 1,797,175 barrels while the Red River area's grew to 6,802,349 barrels. In 1916, however, De Soto–Red River's production began to fall, a trend that continued, with the exception of 1919 and 1920, when production rose temporarily to 4,100,000 barrels and 5,923,000 barrels, respectively. By 1947 the entire field's yearly production had fallen to 273,000 barrels.

Located in Sabine Parish, the Zwolle Field was known from the earliest days of settlement for its oil seeps, and beginning in 1911, twenty-one wells were drilled in the vicinity over the next seventeen years. Not until R. L. Gay completed a well on the Bowman-Hicks Lumber Company lease in the Blue Lake District, however, did active development begin. Completed to a depth of 2,130 feet, Gay's well initially flowed at a rate of fifty barrels per day. Although this was hardly sufficient to start a rush to the area, another well, the Bowman-Hicks Lumber Company No. A-1, located about twelve miles east of the Blue Lake District, was completed on November 26, 1929, as a four-thousand-barrel-per-day producer through a partly closed master gate valve.

This strike brought other oil men hurrying to the area, and several other wells soon were underway. The D. M. Lide *et al.* Sabine Lumber Company No. 1 was completed about three-quarters of a mile from Zwolle on February 11, 1930, with an initial production of eleven hundred barrels a day. Within a short time forty wells were spudded in nearby. Later, in May, 1930, the Pelican Natural Gas Company expanded the field about five miles to the east of the discovery well when it completed its Louisiana Long Leaf Lumber Company No. 1. Drilling continued in all directions, with new wells being sunk 330 feet from property lines, or 660 feet apart, as long as production could be found.

Zwolle's production continued to grow steadily until by December, 1932, the field contained 142 wells with an average daily production of 8,345 barrels of crude. Total cumulative production to that time amounted to 7,339,408 barrels of oil. That same month, on December 5, acid treatment was begun in an effort to increase the field's production. The process entailed forcing acid into the producing formations to break them down and allow more oil to be recovered. The first experiment was on the Sabine Production Company's Pearce No. 1. Before treatment the well had produced nearly ninety thousand barrels of crude since its completion in November, 1930. At the time of the acid treatment, the No. 1 Pearce was flowing at an average of fifty-five barrels daily. After the treatment, production jumped 100 percent for about a month before declining to the previous level.

Another effort was made on the Louisiana Long Leaf Lumber Company No. 16. Completed on November 2, 1932, the well flowed at an average of only 12 barrels per day. After December 10, 1932, when it was treated with acid, production climbed to 376 barrels in just twelve hours and 666 barrels during the next twenty-four hours. Encouraged by this success, the producers treated the Louisiana Long Leaf Lumber Company No. 14 with acid on December 13. Initial production had been about 10 barrels per day before treatment, but afterward output mounted to 371 barrels daily. Approximately one year after the acid treatments, in December, 1931, the two wells, Nos. 14 and 16, had a daily average of 177 and 171 barrels, respectively. Between the time of the acid treatment and January 1, 1934, the wells had produced a total of 226,763 barrels of crude.

The expansion of the field and experiments with acid treatment continued to drive up the field's production figures. By December, 1933, the field's cumulative output of oil amounted to 10,266,896 barrels. By January, 1934, the Zwolle Field's proven boundaries stretched twenty-two miles in an east-west direction, with a maximum width of four miles. By January 1 of that year a total of 623 wells had been sunk in the pool. Of that number, 262 were producers.

Another important strike was made in Claiborne Parish, Louisiana. The Haynesville Field, in the northwestern part of that parish, is just west-northwest of the town from which it draws its name. The rush to the area began in 1918 when oil was discovered at Homer, just southeast of Haynesville. By August, 1918, the area was being extensively examined for additional deposits.

Roxana Petroleum Company was one of the early developers of the area. In August, 1919, the company purchased a half-interest in a twenty-five-thousand-acre block of leases and sank two test wells. The first, the Taylor No. 1, was abandoned in November that year at 1,085 feet; the second, the Taylor No. 2, was abandoned in May, 1920, at the 2,904-foot level after showing signs of oil at 2,200 feet. Although its early efforts had not found any significant production, Roxana started two more holes in 1920: the Meadown No. 1 and the Sayles No. 1. Both were abandoned as dusters, and the firm sold all but five hundred acres of its holdings in the region for seventy-five hundred dollars to J. E. and C. B. Smitherman of Shreveport.

The Smitherman brothers decided to rework the Taylor No. 2, but in December, 1920, they abandoned the project as impractical. Next, they drilled another well about 500 feet from the Taylor No. 2, and there they brought in an eight-thousand-barrel-per-day gusher at 2,850 feet on March 30, 1921. The discovery touched off a mad rush for leases in the area; however, extensive overdevelopment was prevented by the Louisiana Conservation Department, which enforced a rule prohibiting drilling within 330 feet of property lines. Eventually production at the Taylor No. 2 stabilized at two thousand barrels of oil daily. The Smitherman brothers eventually sold the leases in the Haynesville vicinity for $3,375,000.

At first the development at Haynesville was limited to the immediate vicinity of the Smitherman brothers' well. However, on July 3, 1921, two wells—the Florsheim *et al.* Goree No. 1 and the Wideman *et al.* Hunt No. 1—expanded the field's development to the south. Afterward, Haynesville was rapidly developed; by December 31, 1921, it was producing 48,487 barrels of oil every twenty-four hours. Unfortunately, because of numerous "line fights" and hastily drilled wells, there were many unnecessary holes drilled and a large amount of waste before the pool's operators agreed to a spacing program that limited wells to one in every ten acres.

Haynesville's location and development were based almost entirely on geological investigation. As a result, the larger oil companies—Ohio Oil Company, Gilliland Oil Company, Louisiana Oil Refining Corporation, and Roxana—controlled nearly 82 percent of the field's acreage. By the end of 1921, the field was undergoing tremendous flush production. One hundred five wells had been completed, and the pool's productive area had been expanded to approximately fifty-five hundred acres. Another 95 wells were being drilled. Under the spacing agreement then in force, an additional 450 wells could be drilled. Initially, the field's wells showed little sign of natural gas.

On December 31, 1921, Haynesville had fifty-eight wells pumping, four being swabbed, thirty-one flowing, and three idle. The average daily production from these ninety-six wells was 434 barrels, and the field's total production to that time amounted to 3,552,122 barrels. Production peaked the following year at 19,939,000 barrels. Eventually the average per-acre yield in the Haynesville Field amounted to 7,366 barrels. After 1922, Haynesville's production began to decline rapidly, dropping to 10,496,000 barrels in 1923 and 6,720,000 barrels in 1924. During the remainder of the 1920s the field's production continued to decline, but more slowly than before, and by the 1930s it had stabilized at between 1,902,000 and 1,064,000 barrels. However, in 1940 the pool's production plunged below the 1,000,000-barrel mark to 987,000 barrels.

In 1942 the Haynesville Field was expanded northward into Arkansas when the Navarro Oil Company completed its S. J. Beene No. 1 at a depth of 5,540 feet. The initial production was 92 barrels daily, and within a short time several other wells were being drilled. By early 1946 the Arkansas portion of the Haynesville Field contained thirty-three wells. Production for that area peaked in May, 1945, with a monthly output of 71,316 barrels of crude and 128,892,000,000 cubic feet of natural gas. Afterward, production in the Arkansas part of the field began to decline. However, by mid-1946 Arkansas' contribution to Haynesville's production totaled 1,670,246 barrels of oil and 2,728,901 million cubic feet of natural gas.

With the expansion of the Haynesville Field across the border into Arkansas, production began to rise. By 1942, Haynesville's total output had grown to 4,621,000 barrels; the following year it reached 5,368,000 barrels before beginning another slow decline. Production for 1944, 1945, and 1946 was 3,816,000, 2,356,000, and 2,936,000 barrels, respectively. In 1947 the field's total production was 3,099,000 barrels of oil.

The Homer Field proved to be "the most prolific, and . . . the most profitable of the northern Louisiana oil fields" to that time. Located twelve miles south of the Haynesville Field, it contained twenty-three hundred acres of productive land with a diameter of approximately nine miles. Development of the field began in 1916 when A. E. Wilder, on the recommendation of John Y. Smyder, leased thirty thousand acres of land in the region. In November of that year, Wilder assigned fifteen thousand acres of the land to the Atlas Oil Company (which later became the Palmer Corporation), provided that drilling on the tract begin before February 2, 1917. A. E. Hartman, the Atlas Oil Company geologist, examined the lease and suggested that a test well be drilled on section 20, township 21 north, range 7 west. However, Hartman left the company before work on the well began, and the test well, the Moore No. 1, was moved to section 22, T21N, R7W. It was abandoned as dry at 2,910 feet.

In August, 1917, the Atlas Company assigned two blocks of leases, one of 3,753 acres and the other of 3,879 acres, to T. F. Denman and A. F. Williams, who agreed to sink one test well on each block. In November of that year the Consolidated Progressive Oil Company acquired Denman's and Williams's leases and began drilling the holes. The first well, the Featherstone No. 1, was sunk near Hartman's original location. The well was abandoned at 2,287 feet after yielding only a show of oil. On January 12, 1919, the second well was spudded in on the Shaw farm. Drilled to between 1,409 and 1,416 feet, the well produced twenty-five hundred barrels of oil and water every twenty-four hours.

On June 30, 1919, the Homer Field was expanded northward when the Standard Oil Company's Lowenbert No. 1 was opened as a 150-barrel-per-day producer from the Nacatoch sand at a depth of 1,160 feet. On October 10, 1920, the Standard Oil Company's Guy Oaks No. 1, hit the Oakes sand at the 2,090-foot level; it blew in at twenty thousand barrels per day. Homer's wells were characterized by a high initial daily production, one well initially flowing at forty thousand barrels every twenty-four hours from the Oakes sand.

Eventually the Homer Pool was divided into the north field, with 2,280 acres of proven production, and the south field, containing 1,030 acres of production. By 1929, the number of wells drilled in the north field was 295, with 337 in the south field. All wells in the north field were completed to the Nacatoch sand, with an average spacing of 4.3 acres per well. In the south field 198 wells were completed to the Nacatoch sand, and 129 wells were drilled to the Oakes sand.

The Homer Field was rapidly developed. In May, 1919, the field's output was 10,034 barrels per day, but by December of that year production had jumped to 879,960 barrels every twenty-four hours. Homer's production peaked in 1920 when the pool produced 21,508,000 barrels of Louisiana's total annual production of 35,714,000 barrels. That same month also witnessed the pool's highest daily average: 79,894 barrels.

Homer's production soon dropped dramatically, however, falling to 12,182,836 barrels in 1921 and 6,293,809 barrels in 1922. Beginning in 1927, the pool's output dipped below the 2,000,000-barrel mark for the first time. By January 1, 1928, the Homer Field contained 482 wells with an average daily production of 9 barrels per well, for a total of 4,360 barrels of crude every twenty-four hours. Per-acre production yield to that time was 24,500 barrels.

By 1933, Homer's annual production fell to less than 1,000,000 barrels, but its total accumulated production amounted to 64,500,000 barrels, the second highest in the state up to that time. Then began a gradual increase followed by a slow decline. By 1947 production had dropped to 915,000 barrels.

Another important strike was made at the Cotton Valley Field, located in Webster Parish, Louisiana, approximately forty miles northeast of Shreveport and twelve miles west of the Homer Field. Oil men first began to notice the region when gas was discovered there in the "Blossom" sand in August, 1922, and oil was uncovered in October, 1923. An extensive drilling program soon began, and by 1924 the field was producing 1,211,000 barrels of crude, but the early development of the field was confined mainly to a narrow productive area encircling the central part of the field, which contained gas. Development of the "Blossom" sand was rapid, but by 1928, water composed 90 percent of the gross fluid production from this horizon. By 1929 the "Blossom" sand formation would yield approximately 11,500,000 barrels of crude.

Cotton Valley's other production came from deep horizons. The first well producing from the Trinity group, which included the Upper Trinity red series, the Glen Rose formations, and the Lower Trinity red series, came in at a depth of approximately 3,300 feet. Completed in the Glen Rose anhydrite gas horizon by the Palmer Corporation in February, 1926, the well led to the drilling of other gas wells in the Cotton Valley Field. Not until the Ohio Oil Company completed its Bodcaw No. 38 in April, 1928, however, were the deep horizons opened to oil production. The Bodcaw No. 38 initially flowed at a rate of between 3,000 and 4,000 barrels of crude daily from a twelve-foot-thick sand at the 4,669-foot level. An offshoot, the Bodcaw No. 39, then was drilled, and the two wells produced approximately 320,000 barrels of oil before going to water.

By 1925, Cotton Valley's output had climbed to 3,348,000 barrels of crude, but that was the field's highest point for twelve years, as production began a slow decline. At the beginning of the 1930s, Cotton Valley's production had dropped to 880,000 barrels of crude, and it would continue to fall until it reached a low of 207,000 barrels in 1936.

The temendous depth of the field's wells delayed development, but in the late 1930s Cotton Valley began to make a comeback. In 1939, the field reached it peak with an output of 5,189,000 barrels of crude. Afterward, production again began a slow decrease. By 1944, Cotton Valley's output had slumped to 724,000 barrels, and the next year it dipped to 388,000. Then the field underwent another dramatic jump in production as output climbed to 2,671,000 barrels in 1946.

Yet another major field, the Urania, is located in northern Louisiana. Although the main part of the pool is in LaSalle Parish, the field also extends into Grant and Winn parishes. The producing area, approximately three miles wide and ten miles long, is about one hundred miles southeast of Shreveport and fifty miles south of Monroe. The field is divided into two districts: the Tullos-Urania District in the north, and the Georgetown District in the south.

Development in the area began in late 1924 and early 1925 when the Urania Petroleum Company sank five wells in LaSalle Parish, and all yielded shows of oil. Encouraged, officials of the company began work on a sixth well, the Urania Lumber Company No. 6. Located by H. G. Schneider and W. R. Julian, the well was completed on March 25, 1925, as an eight-hundred-barrel-per-day producer. However, it flowed for only seven hours before sanding up. Attempts were made to clean and repair the hole, but they were unsuccessful, and the well was abandoned.

In August, 1925, the Urania Petroleum Company completed its Urania Lumber Company No. 7 as a ten-barrel-per-day producer. Although it was a producer, the well's low output did not cause much excitement, and activity in the Urania area lagged. However, in September of that year, the Beckman and Freeman No. 2 well several miles away blew out and cratered at a depth of one thousand feet. Though in 1925 the field's total production was only about ten thousand barrels of oil, this amount was enough to cause oil men to again take notice of the region, and development of the Urania Field began at a rapid pace.

By February, 1926, 31 wells had been completed in the pool, with an average daily production of 62.5 barrels per well—a total output of 1,939 barrels of crude every twenty-four hours. However, the number of wells more than doubled to 68 by the following month. Likewise, the average daily production per well jumped to nearly 92 barrels, or a total of 6,239 barrels every day. Urania's number of wells continued to increase over the following months until it peaked in May, 1927, at 365. At the same time, the field's average daily production jumped to 16,585 barrels in October, 1926—the largest daily production of any Louisiana oil field at that time. That same month's total production amounted to 514,135 barrels of crude. By September 1, 1927, the total production of the Urania Field was 6,588,819 barrels.

Little gas was found with the oil in Urania, and wells there did not flow long. Rotary drilling was used entirely in the development of the pool, and the average well was completed in from four to twelve days. The common practice was to begin the hole with a fifteen-inch bit and sink in to the 100- to 150-foot level, where ten-inch casing was set to exclude the surface water.

Water proved to be one of Urania's biggest drawbacks. Most of the sand carried water, and when it was added to the bottom water, it presented a great problem. Most of the field's wells had an initial water content ranging from 10 to 30 percent of the total fluid, but this initial percentage rapidly increased until the fluid stabilized at 85 percent water and 15 percent oil. The presence of such a large volume of water and emulsion with the oil required dehydration, and because of a lack of pipelines into the field, it was necessary to haul the production by railroad tank cars to refineries. The water problem was greatest in the Georgetown District, where wells initially produced approximately 90 percent water and 10 percent oil, with the water increasing so rapidly that most wells were abandoned as unprofitable soon after they were completed. As a result, the total output of the Georgetown District was disappointing, amounting to only about 75,000 barrels by March, 1927. Through September 1, 1927, the entire pool produced 1,650 barrels of oil per acre from approximately thirty-nine hundred oil-bearing acres.

Urania's output peaked in 1926, when production was 3,669,000 barrels of oil. Afterward, it slowly declined. In 1930, Urania's output dipped below the 2,000,000-barrel level, holding at about half that figure annually until 1938. In 1939 production decreased to 974,000 barrels, and the slide downward continued; by 1946 the Urania Field was producing only about 601,000 barrels of crude annually.

The opening of the Urania Field led to an extensive exploration program along the Angelina-Caldwell Flexure. In 1926, a total of 225 wildcat wells were drilled along this formation alone. Unfortunately, no additional oil production was discovered; however, this exploration did lead to the location of the Richland gas field to the northeast in Richland Parish.

Yet of all the strikes made in northern Louisiana, the Monroe gas field was so large that it was considered a separate entity by oil men.

Left: This small, relatively flimsy derrick in the Bossier Field about 1920 was sufficient for the shallow production found in the early pools in the parish. *Louisiana State Library*. *Right*: Fighting a burning gas well, the Nelson No. 1, at Bull Bayou, Sabine Parish, in the early 1920s. The workers are attempting to spray water from steam boilers on the blaze, apparently with little effect. *Louisiana State Library*.

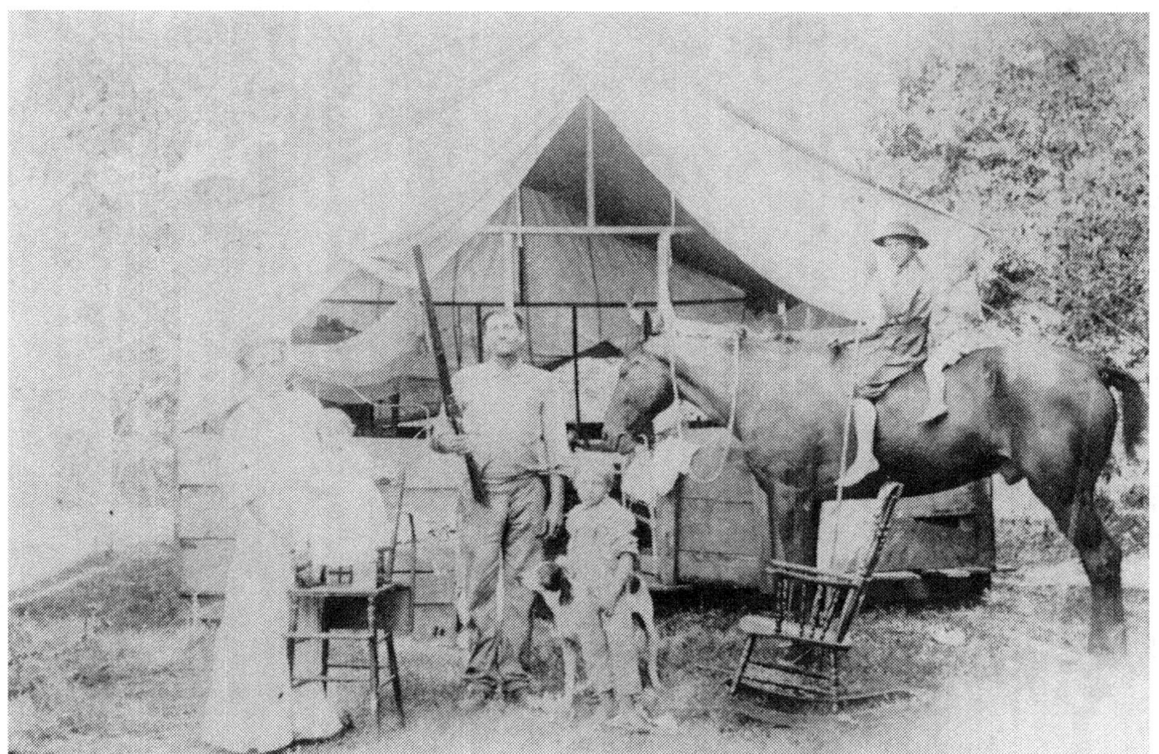

This tent, labeled Graham's Camp, sheltered the family of an oil worker somewhere in northern Louisiana. Many of the men who followed the booms with their families could not find adequate housing and lived in tents. Boards used as a floor and sidewalls gave the tent a little more permanency and kept out wild hogs raiding for food. *Jack Norman*.

The Haynesville Field in Clayborne Parish had many difficult roads. Here, a mule team is attempting to pull a wagon through a mud bog with encouragement from a whip-wielding man to the right of the wagon. The mule at the left rear of the team is sunk completely above his hindquarters in the mud. *Mark Stewart and Eugene Spruell.*

A frustrated driver in the oil fields of northern Louisiana. This man was stuck in a mud bog in the northern part of Bossier Parish on March 12, 1922. The photographer noted on the back of the photograph that the automobile was bogged down to its front axle in the mud, its battery was too weak to turn the motor, and the driver could splash water in his face by trying to start it with the crank. *Mark Stewart and Eugene Spruell.*

This delivery cart belonging to the Lakela Iron Works—a drill-bit dressing shop in Haynesville—was improvised to cope with the muddy roads of the area. It was made of a front axle, a pair of hind wheels, and a box. The tongue is stiff, and a pair of mules furnished the "horsepower." *Mark Stewart and Eugene Spruell.*

The boom town of Haynesville in 1920. The two cafés seem to be particularly crowded, and the entire community is alive with the commercial activity generated by the boom. Only one woman is visible in the entire scene. *W. B. Grabill.*

Left: A gusher owned by the Rowe Oil Company in the Homer area. The well blew in on September 9, 1919, initially producing thirty thousand barrels per day at 2,091 feet. *Louisiana State Library*. *Right*: Another spectacular gusher in the Homer Field in the early 1920s. This particular well tapped the Blossom sand at 2,095 feet and initially flowed at approximately thirty thousand barrels per day. *Louisiana State Library*.

A drilling crew in northwestern Louisiana in about 1920. Although the exact location is not known, it probably was in the Homer area. *Louisiana State Library*.

The Gladys-Bell Oil Company's Featherstone No. 1 in the Homer Field. The well struck a paying sand at 1,143 feet. *Louisiana State Library.*

The Homer Field also was the scene of terrible roads. Here, a twenty-mule team attempts to haul a boiler to the fields, but the boiler wagon is bogged down to the rear axle within the city limits of Homer in front of some fashionable homes. *Graydon F. Smart*, Sheveport Magazine.

Another view of the Homer Field in the early 1920s. Note the lean-to in the foreground to provide some shelter for the workers and the stack of casing pipe to the left of the derrick. At the far right is a tent used to house some of the workers on the lease. *Louisiana State Library*.

The Austin Oil Company's Oakes lease near Homer in the early 1920s. Note the numerous pipes on top of the ground feeding crude oil from the wells to the storage tanks. *W. B. Grabill.*

Closely spaced derricks on the Austin Oil Company's Oakes lease in the Homer Field. The two derricks in the foreground likely were tapping simultaneously the Nacatoch sand and the Oakes sand. *W. B. Grabill.*

A battery of storage tanks owned by the Gilliland & Foster Oil Company of Homer in the early 1920s. The well behind the tanks in the center of the photo is the Gilliland & Foster Oakes No. 8, which produced five thousand barrels per day. *Louisiana State Library.*

An earthen storage pit near Homer. Note the pipe in the left foreground feeding crude into the lake. *Mark Stewart and Eugene Spruell.*

Left: As northern Louisiana's boom got underway, it was necessary to construct adequate pipelines to carry the oil and natural gas to markets. Laying pipelines through the thick undergrowth was not easy. However, by 1919 the Interstate Oil Pipeline Company of Shreveport had several lines under construction in the region. After the pipe was lowered into the ditch, wooden forms were constructed around it, and the forms were then filled with cement to protect the metal pipe from corrosion. *Penn-Well Publishing Company*. *Right*: E. T. ("Reb") Oakes, discoverer of the Lisbon Field in Clayborne Parish, is shown here in 1941, five years after bringing in the field. *Pictoral Trade Journal of the Petroleum Industry*.

Reb Oakes directs crude from the discovery well of the Lisbon Field into an earthen storage pit while an interested crowd of spectators observes. *W. B. Grabill*.

R. O. Roy at the site of his No. 1-E Farmer, a wildcat well in DeSoto Parish that he had just completed in 1930. It flowed at the rate of 2,500 barrels daily. In 1921, Roy had uncovered the prolific Bellevue Shallow Field in Bossier Parish. With him is W. H. Farmer, a Mansfield, Louisiana, banker and fee owner of the land on which the well was located. *PennWell Publishing Company.*

The Texas Company's pumping station at Crichton, Louisiana. *Estate of M. Carl Jones.*

Left: The Great Depression ended for D. E. Stephens in 1932 when oil was discovered on his 720-acre tract of land in Sabine Parish. *PennWell Publishing Company*. *Right*: A rotary rig in action in the Lisbon Pool in 1941. Here, the drillers are attaching new drill pipe at the Union Producing Company No. 1-A Meadows, a deep-test well north of the Lisbon Field. Note the drill pipe stacked inside the derrick behind the men. The well at this point had reached 10,393 feet and was continuing deeper. *PennWell Publishing Company*.

The Giles No. 2 gas well blowing wild near Springhill, Louisiana, in Webster Parish near the Arkansas border on March 11, 1922. The drillers faced a dilemma, because they knew if they were to close the valve, the hole would blow out under the six-inch line and they possibly could lose the entire well. *Mark Stewart and Eugene Spruell*.

A lease near Tullos, Louisiana, in October, 1926. The man on the left is identified as John R. Sibley. *Irma Tucker.*

Street scene in the boom town of Cotton Valley in Webster Parish in 1936. At the left is the S.S. Cafe, and at the center is Red Sims's Cafe. Two establishments down the street prominently display signs advertising a popular beer. *PennWell Publishing Company.*

Left: The tremendous gas pressures encountered in the Cotton Valley Field caused many wells to blow out and some to crater, creating spectacular geysers like this one in 1937. *PennWell Publishing Company*. *Right*: A massive, seven-thousand-pound Christmas tree was hooked up to the Cotton Valley deep gas discovery well in 1936. *PennWell Publishing Company*.

Two offset wells race for production in 1936 in a classic lease-line fight just south of the Miller County, Arkansas, line. The well on the left is ready for casing to be cemented. *PennWell Publishing Company*.

Another nothern Louisiana gas field featuring tremendous pressure was the Sligo Field in Bossier Parish. Here, at the Triangle Drilling Company's No. 1-E Skannal, 634 feet of 4½-inch drilling pipe were thrown from the well by natural gas flowing wild. One end of the string of pipe hangs over the crown block of the derrick, while the other end loops around the foreground to disappear into the wooded area at the left. The gasser is blowing wide open while workmen wet the rig to prevent a fire. *PennWell Publishing Company.*

An Arkansas Fuel Company gas well coming in in the Sligo Field. *Cities Service.*

The Industrial Gas Company's No. 1 Earle in the Richland Parish gas field. This well had an open flow of 39,535,540 cubic feet of gas in 1929. *PennWell Publishing Company.*

A double-pressure weathering system at the Alto, Louisiana, natural gasoline plant in the Richland Parish Field in 1929. Such operations were commonplace in many of the gas fields of Louisiana and southern Arkansas. They extracted distillates, including natural gasoline used for motor fuel, from the natural gas. *PennWell Publishing Company.*

The Spyker No. 1, discovery well of the Monroe gas rock formation, with a crowd of visitors on June 28, 1916, the day the well was spudded in on the plantation of Leonodis Pendleton Spyker, three to five miles south of Bastrop, Louisiana. In recent years the plantation became the property of Northeast Louisiana University, and it contained seventy-five to one hundred producing wells in 1981. *Sandel Library, Northeast Louisiana University.*

LOCATED in Ouachita, Morehouse, and Union parishes, the Monroe gas field stretches from about seven miles northeast of the city of Monroe to approximately six miles northwest of Bastrop. In 1901 Green B. Haynes, Sr., a sawmill owner and timber broker, began a well near Cheniere. Drilled by a cable-tool rig under the supervision of A. F. Middaugh, the well reached four hundred feet before cave-ins resulting from the encroachment of water caused the operations to cease for a time. Haynes later obtained a rotary drilling rig and began to deepen the hole. At nine hundred feet he encountered a small pocket of natural gas.

Although this strike created quite a bit of excitement among area residents, who rushed to the well site to view the "gusher," most of the crowd returned home once it became obvious that no oil had been found. Determined to find crude, Green again decided to deepen the hole and pushed the bit to approximately thirteen hundred feet, where casing was set. Unfortunately, the well's drill stem was twisted off, and after repeated unsuccessful efforts to retrieve the tools, the hole was abandoned.

By 1906, blowouts were common along the Ouachita River, especially near the Old Breard Shingle Mill on North Riverfront Street in Monroe, where the natural gas would often catch fire and burn for extended lengths of time. However, actual development in the area did not begin until 1909, when a well was drilled in the Monroe City Park. Some natural gas was encountered at the 1,300-foot level, but at 1,500 feet the bit hit saltwater. In 1910 a well was sunk in Forsythe Park by Dr. A. A. Forsythe, who at the time was mayor of Monroe. At 2,350 feet the bit penetrated a saltwater layer containing natural gas. After the water and gas were separated, the water was pumped into a nearby swimming pool, and the natural gas was used to light the park and heat water in the bathhouse. Two nearby residents, Joe Beidenharn and Joe Mangham, also piped the gas into their homes for personal use.

These efforts heightened interest in the region, and in late part of 1910 and early 1911 the Consolidated Ice Company, under the direction of E. C. Fudicker, sank another well in the region. A little gas was encountered, and six other wells were drilled in hopes of increasing production. Later, in 1914, the ice company completed its Fee No. 6 inside the Monroe city limits. Both gas and saltwater were found between 1,251 and 1,264 feet and also between 1,144 and 1,146 feet.

That same year, 1914, R. R. Bondurant, W. B. Clark, O. B. Morton, H. J. Trousdale, H. G. Prophet, G. G. Weaks, J. E. Morgan, and W. H. Morgan formed the Monroe Oil and Gas Company. After selling stock, they began a well just north of Monroe in the Fairview addition. Bondurant and his two sons oversaw the drilling, but at eight hundred feet the drill stem twisted off. Their bad luck continued, and several months were necessary to sink the hole to eighteen hundred feet, where the well was abandoned after the stem again was twisted off and they were unable to fish it out of the hole.

Shortly afterward, Louis Lock of Monroe began leasing acreage in the vicinity. With the help of J. H. Hampton, he accumulated 13,500 acres by early 1916. One-half of the property was sold to Louis Cosper, and shortly afterward the two oil men contracted with C. E. Fauntleroy to construct a 60-foot derrick on one of their leases. Later they employed R. E. ("Lucky Bob") Allison, a Texas driller, to sink the well. When Allison arrived at the drilling site, he promptly declared the original structure insufficient to support the weight of drilling tools. Only a 112-foot derrick would suffice.

Determined to begin anew, Lock threw a half-dollar into the air, declared the spot where it landed to be a "gas bump," and ordered the new derrick erected on the site. Work on the derrick began on June 10, 1916, and the well, the Spyker No. 1, was spudded in eighteen days later on June 28.

Everything went well until it became necessary to set eight-inch casing. Lock, Hampton, and Cosper did not have the five thousand dollars needed to pay for the job. To raise the money, the three original owners formed the Progressive Oil & Gas Company with George G. Weaks, J. H. Trousdale, H. G. Prophet, Travis Oliver, Carl McHenry, Eugere Wolff, and J. T. Hampton. Sufficient money was raised to continue drilling operations, but more cash was needed. They decided to continue drilling until they either reached 3,000 feet or struck oil or natural gas in excess of two million cubic feet and then sell stock to raise more money. At 2,275 feet a huge pocket of natural gas was found, with enough pressure almost to blow the drill stem out of the hole. Immediately a pipe was laid about one hundred feet from the wellhead, and the gas was lit.

The strike generated quite a bit of excitement. The local railway ran special trains to Monroe to handle the sightseers, and the Progressive Oil & Gas Company had little trouble in selling stock. An open-flow test on September 3, 1916, recorded 2,500,000 cubic feet per day. The gas rock was nearly 50 feet thick, but at 2,902 feet, warm saltwater was struck, and the well was abandoned. Almost immediately the company started another well, the Fisher No. 1, two miles to the north. Completed in October, 1916, the Fisher No. 1 produced almost 5,212,000 cubic feet of natural gas per day from 2,255 feet. Production later stabilized at about 3,000,000 cubic feet daily.

Several other wells were started in 1916, extending the producing area of the field along an eight-mile stretch and expanding it into Ouachita Parish late in the year when the Ouachita Oil and Natural Gas Company completed its A. L. Smith No. 1 near Sterlington. Initial flow of that well measured 6,431,000 cubic feet per day.

In 1917, thirteen wells were drilled in the Monroe area. One of them, the Lieber No. 1, produced an open-flow capacity of 21,000,000 cubic feet per day. In the following year the Monroe Field was extended several miles to the west as eighteen more wells were drilled.

The tremendous gas pressure in the Monroe Field caused extensive problems for drillers. Blowouts were common and generally cratered the well. When this happened, the entire rig might be swallowed up. Another problem appeared on March 16, 1919, when the Sandridge No. 1 at 561 feet hit an artesian freshwater sand heavily charged with gas. Gas and water both blew over the top of the derrick as the well cratered, and the mixture of mud and water in the crater continued to be churned by the gas until it resembled a bubbling caldron. In the summer of 1921, the Sandridge No. 1 was still spewing gas and water, and the crater had grown to a diameter of 125 feet.

The Monroe Field was filled with wild wells. The No. 3 Smith was completed and capped on November 10, 1918, but not until September 16, 1919, was the well opened. Its initial flow was at a rate of 10,350,000 cubic feet of gas per day, but within a few minutes it appeared that the hole had bridged over. Suddenly it began spewing large pieces of rock, and again it was quickly shut down. About three days later, gas began leaking at the top of the casing. By November, 1919, a small crater had formed under the derrick, and on the fifteenth of that month the hole was filled with dirt. Gas blew out again on December 27, 1919, and by January 4, 1920, the casing had settled; the crater had undermined the derrick, and the well was abandoned. Water and the timber from the derrick washed against the sides of the crater, and the hole grew rapidly. About April 20, 1920, the ground between the well and the nearby bayou began to form into small craters. By the summer of 1921 the main crater was two hundred feet in diameter, and small craters extended a full two hundred feet from the well to the bayou.

Although cursed with blowouts and cratering wells, oil men continued to expand the Monroe Field. By April 1, 1921, there were eighty-eight wells within the pool's area of proven production. Of these, sixty-five were gas wells, seven were being drilled, three were bridged over, six had been abandoned, four were wild crater wells, one was blowing wild, and two were producing saltwater and gas with no effort being made to retrieve the gas.

Between March 1, 1920, and March 1, 1921, the Monroe Field produced a total of 21,445,000,000 cubic feet of gas, and by February, 1921, the field's average daily production was 77,840,000 cubic feet. However, that month the wells were operating only at 24 percent of their open-flow capability. Had the valves been opened all the way, Monroe was capable of producing 324,507,000 cubic feet daily. Moreover, because of high gas pressure and frequent blowouts, there was a large amount of waste. It was estimated that the Smith No. 1 spewed 2,500,000 cubic feet of natural gas per day into the air, and another well, the Guthrie No. 1, blew 300,000,000 cubic feet per day into the atmosphere.

Production continued to mount during the 1920s. Twenty-three wells were completed in 1921, an additional 42 the following year, 120 in 1923, and 109 in 1924. By the mid-1920s the Monroe Field was recognized as the "world's greatest gas field."

Because of the great concentration of natural gas at Monroe, the field became a center of production of carbon black, which was used in the manufacture of rubber, printing ink, stove polish, phonograph records, and so on. The Southern Carbon Company of Charleston, West Virginia, opened a plant in the Monroe Field in 1917. By April 1, 1921, there were nine carbon black plants in the Monroe Field. Six were operating in conjunction with plants that produced gasoline from the gas. Their total daily production amounted to seventy-eight hundred gallons of gasoline and seventy-one thousand pounds of carbon black from 91.3 percent of the field's natural gas production. Monroe's natural gas also was being piped into area homes and businesses, but this use accounted for only 5.8 percent of the field's production. The going rate for Monroe's gas in February, 1921, was two cents per thousand cubic feet.

Peak production was reached in 1924. Agitation to limit the burning of natural gas to produce carbon black prompted the Louisiana State Conservation Commission to order the Monroe Field's production cut 35 percent, resulting in the closing of several carbon plants. There being no other market for surplus natural gas, activity in the field slowed. However, once it became practical to generate electricity with natural gas, the Louisiana Power and Light Company built a huge generating plant near Sterlington, and production resumed. Later, several pipelines tapped the field and pumped Monroe's gas to Missouri, Tennessee, Alabama, Louisiana, and Texas. To expand the field's market, the first all-welded natural gas pipeline was constructed from Monroe to huge refinery complexes at Beaumont and Port Arthur, Texas.

Two other nearby gas fields, Elm Grove and Richland, also were uncovered. The Elm Grove gas field, at first thought to be part of the huge Monroe Field, is located about twenty miles south of Shreveport in Bossier Parish. The Atlas Oil Company located it in 1916, and within a year production from Elm Grove had been expanded to cover portions of five northeastern Louisiana parishes. Ten years later, in 1926, the Richland gas field was discovered just to the east of Monroe in Richland Parish. It was eventually expanded to cover 42,240 acres. Both these later finds were completely overshadowed by Monroe's huge output.

By 1924, largely as a result of the massive production of the Monroe and Caddo Lake fields, two "all-inclusive" conservation statutes were passed by Louisiana's legislature—one for natural gas and the other for oil. Although Louisiana legislators had taken the lead in the conservation of oil and natural gas, federal officials began to threaten to increase their regulatory powers. On June 10, 1929, President Herbert Hoover assembled an Oil Conservation Congress at the Broadmoor Hotel in Colorado Springs, Colorado, to discuss the problem of waste and overproduction and the possibility of federal regulation. Faced with this threat, many independent producers met the following day at the Antlers Hotel and organized the Independent Petroleum Association of America or the IPAA. Louisiana oil men were active in the IPAA and supported its goals, among which was a drive to limit imported oil, and between 1945 and 1947, B. A. Hardey of Shreveport served as president of the organization.

Although Louisiana officials had taken an early interest in the conservation of oil and natural gas, by the early 1930s some abuses still existed, and the federal government again threatened to intervene. Under Franklin D. Roosevelt's administration the passage of Section 9c of the National Industrial Recovery Act, and the president's executive order affirming the right of the federal government to regulate overproduction, once again thrust federal regulation onto the region's oil men.

About that same time E. W. Marland, governor of Oklahoma and an oil man himself, issued a call for representatives of the oil-producing states to gather at Ponca City, Oklahoma, in early December, 1934, to undertake their own conservation program. Faced with increased federal involvement, Louisiana dispatched representatives to the gathering, and in January, 1935, when the Interstate Oil Compact Commission (IOCC) was actually organized, both John S. Farrell and Ralph H. Cummings were present to represent Louisiana's interests. Nevertheless, the state did not immediately join the IOCC.

In 1936, Louisiana's solons modified the state's conservation laws along the lines of New Mexico's, which at the time were considered the most advanced in existence. Four years later, in 1940, Louisiana passed one of the most comprehensive oil codes ever enacted. Production limits were based on the prevention of waste and not upon "reasonable market demand"; the protection of the correlative rights of all co-owners of property subject to regulation were outlined; proper spacing regulations to eliminate unnecessary drilling were drafted; and the IOCC was authorized to regulate recycling and pressure maintenance programs. The following year, 1941, Louisiana became an active partner in the IOCC.

The Fisher No. 1, the second well drilled by the Progressive Oil and Gas Company of Monroe, Louisiana. The pipe is in the derrick ready to be set for casing, and the well is flowing gas. *Sandel Library, Northeast Louisiana University.*

Another view of the Fisher No. 1, with the Progressive Oil and Gas Company stockholders, the drilling contractor, and a visitor on a derrick floor. *Left to right*: Lewis H. Cosper, L. K. Skikivith, Carl McHenry, Louis Lock, George G. Weaks, Eugene Wolff, R. E. ("Lucky Bob") Allison (drilling contractor), and J. H. Hampton (visitor). *Sandel Library, Northeast Louisiana University.*

One of drilling contractor Fred Stovall's early rigs spudding in a well in the Monroe Gas Field about 1918. Stovall, who drilled many wells in the field, mounted his pole rig on a wagon that could be hauled to the well site and powered by tractors. *Fred Stovall Collection, Sandel Library, Northeast Louisiana University.*

Fred Stovall's wagon-mounted rotary drilling rig. *Fred Stovall Collection, Sandel Library, Northeast Louisiana University.*

Fred Stovall (*third from right*) and one of his drilling crews in the Monroe Gas Field. *Fred Stovall Collection, Sandel Library, Northeast Louisiana University.*

Saltwater in the Monroe Gas Field was vented onto the open ground. The problem of what to do with saltwater was often solved this way in the early oil fields. Of course this practice effectively ruined the land for cultivation. Evidences of these saltwater runs may yet be seen in areas of some of the older fields in Louisiana and Arkansas. Eventually conservation legislation, as well as practices initiated by the oil men themselves, brought about less destructive means of saltwater disposal. *Fred Stovall Collection, Sandel Library, Northeast Louisiana University.*

By the mid-1920s, the Monroe Gas Field was considered to be the world's greatest gas field. This photograph shows the master gate on a big gas well somewhere in the Monroe Field in February, 1925. The eyebolts holding the master gate in place were embedded in a cube of concrete approximately eighteen feet on a side to withstand the great gas pressure of the well. *Mark Stewart and Eugene Spruell.*

At another gas well somewhere in the Monroe Field, the various high-pressure lines are buried, but a rock and sections of pipe are being used as a regulator. *Mark Stewart and Eugene Spruell.*

Pipeliners checking for leaks in a gas line between Lamkins in northeastern Louisiana and Hodge, forty-five miles to the southwest. The line had 650 pounds of gas pressure on it, and the workers were happy to find no bubbles indicating a leak. *PennWell Publishing Company.*

Absorbers of a natural gasoline plant at Fowler, Louisiana, operated by the Southern Carbon Company, as they appeared in 1928. *PennWell Publishing Company.*

Company-owned dwellings at the Munce Compressor Station, operated by the Arkansas-Louisiana Gas Company near Sterlington, Louisiana. This camp, pictured here in November, 1934, was one of the finest oil-field camps in the region. Men who were sufficiently fortunate to be able to live in such a camp, as opposed to the oil boom towns, were lucky indeed. *Cities Service.*

The conveying system and power drives of the Imperial Oil and Gas Products Company plant at Sterlington. This apparatus carried carbon black from the burners to the packing units. *PennWell Publishing Company.*

An Arkansas-Louisiana Gas Company gas well in Lincoln Parish, Louisiana, in the 1940s. *Cities Service.*

An acidizing operation in the Monroe Field in 1941. Here, the so-called gas-loading method was used. The well was pressurized, the acid was siphoned in, and compressed gas was employed behind the acid to force it into the formation. More than ninety-six tank cars of acid were used in this particular Monroe operation. Acidizing was one technique used to stimulate and increase production in older fields. *PennWell Publishing Company.*

Governor Sam H. Jones of Louisiana signs the Interstate Oil Compact while Governor Leon C. Phillips of Oklahoma looks over his shoulder. Louisiana joined the IOCC for a trial period in 1941, with renewal of the membership to take place on the condition that other members of the compact bring their conservation standards up to those that Louisiana had in force by 1941. *PennWell Publishing Company.*

The Busey No. 1, discovery well of the El Dorado Field, blows in on January 10, 1921, one mile south of El Dorado, Arkansas. The well, located in the middle of a cotton patch, initially produced between fifteen million and thirty-five million cubic feet of natural gas and ten thousand barrels of top-grade crude per day. Although the well was short-lived, the Busey No. 1 ignited a major rush of oil finders to the new Arkansas oil bonanza. *Eunice Spence Collection, Arkansas Oil Heritage Center.*

FOR several years after the discovery of vast pools of oil in neighboring Louisiana and Oklahoma, oil men had examined south-central Arkansas in search of crude. Most local residents paid scant attention to the prospectors, for before the Roaring Twenties little oil had been found in Arkansas. In 1910, forty-seven wells had been drilled in the state, but thirty-seven had proved to be gas-producers. Despite the disappointment, the search continued.

In 1914 the Penn-Wyoming Oil Company sank a hole ten miles east of El Dorado, in Union County, and two years later Chance Adams, Charles Murphy, and Ed Jones drilled another near the Columbia County line. Both wells were dry. On April 16, 1920, the Hunter Oil Company of Shreveport, Louisiana, under the direction of Colonel Samuel S. Hunter, completed Arkansas's first oil well two and one-half miles east of Stephens in Ouachita County, just to the north of Union County. Yet nothing had been found near El Dorado to indicate the huge pool of petroleum beneath the land.

As excitement waned, most oil men abandoned the area. Then in 1919, Bruce Hunt borrowed $250 from a friend, Sam Arrendale, and leased 12,522 acres near El Dorado. Relying on the advice of J. J. Victor, a geologist, Hunt contracted with the Constantin Refining Company to sink a test well, the Hill No. 1, just west of El Dorado. The Contantin Company shipped a California heavy rotary drilling rig to El Dorado to do the drilling, but when it arrived it was missing some important parts. Hunt's lease required drilling to begin before December 31, 1919, and it was not until two days before the deadline that the needed equipment was found. The Hill No. 1 was spudded in with less than twenty-four hours remaining on the deadline.

Thereafter the drilling seemed routine. The rig was run during the day and shut down during the night as steady progress was made to the 2,200-foot level. When the bit reached 2,243 feet on April 22, 1920, it penetrated a huge pocket of natural gas in the Nacatoch sand. Gas shot saltwater over the derrick, and the roar could be heard in El Dorado, two and one-half miles away. Although the well's initial production of gas was forty million cubic feet daily, the eight barrels of oil that flowed from the wellhead every twenty-four hours were more important to Hunt.

Little problem was encountered in capping the runaway, but within a short time hundreds of craters pockmarked the ten acres surrounding the well site. Crayfish were asphyxiated in their holes by escaping gas, and water wells and creeks within four miles of the Hill No. 1 began to boil and gurgle as gas seeped to the surface. Many nearby residents refused to drink the water. Finally, on June 13, 1920, a sightseer struck a match near one of the craters and set off an inferno that raged for months before it was finally brought under control.

Hunt's find touched off more drilling. Paul R. Mattocks and Harley R. Hinton leased 350 acres about two miles southeast of El Dorado and then leased 80 acres to Dr. L. G. Mitchell and W. R. Bonham of Homer, Louisiana. Mitchell and Bonham started a well in the summer of 1920. The hole was abandoned at one thousand feet, the derrick was moved over a short distance, and another well was started. The second well was abandoned at nine hundred feet when some machinery fell into the hole and could not be fished out. By that time the partners were beginning to face serious financial problems. Dr. Samuel T. Busey, in exchange for 51 percent of the project, furnished funds to complete the hole, and on November 15, 1920, drilling was resumed. The well was now called the Busey-Mitchell Armstrong No. 1 or, more simply, the Busey No. 1.

The derrick of the Busey No. 1 was clearly visible in El Dorado, and when the Nacatoch sand was reached at 2,233 feet on January 10, 1921, a small crowd gathered to witness the event. Drilling ceased, and bailing operations began. At about 4:30 a deep roar was heard as the bailer was being lifted from its sixth trip into the hole. The rumbling grew, and the ground began to shake. Then with a deafening roar, a thick, black column of gas, oil, and water shot out of the well and drenched the spectators.

Oil men immediately began to take serious notice of the region. The No. 1 Busey's initial yield of natural gas was between fifteen million and thirty-five million cubic feet per day. When the well blew in, it was throwing between three thousand and ten thousand barrels of fluid into the air every day; however, within fifteen days of its completion, the fluid began to turn dark brown as oil began to mix with the water, and by February the well was producing one thousand to fifteen hundred barrels of oil daily. Unfortunately, the well's productive life was only about forty-five days; at the end of March, 1921, it was abandoned.

On March 7, 1921, the Caddo Central Oil & Refining Company's Rogers No. 1 well, about one-half mile from the center of El Dorado, blew in with a daily gas flow of between twenty million and twenty-five million cubic feet. Some problems were encountered in capping the well, and when a thunderstorm swept through the field on March 11, lightning ignited the well. The column of gas became a "roaring volcano." The noise was so great that townspeople were forced to plug their ears with cotton or chewing gum, and nearby houses shook from the convulsing earth. Guards were placed to keep the fire from spreading. Trees were cut down, a wide swath of earth plowed up around the well, and nearby wells shut down. Finally, on March 20, with twenty boilers providing smothering steam, the fire was extinguished.

On March 19, 1922, the Shreveport Producing and Refining company made another strike about a mile to the south which flowed at between fifteen thousand and twenty thousand barrels of crude daily, and the rush was on. On May 7, the El Dorado Natural Gas Company's Frazer No. 1 penetrated the Meakin sand at 2,529 feet. Although the well flowed at ten million cubic feet of natural gas and two thousand barrels of saltwater daily, the formation proved to be a big disappointment. Another deep horizon, in the Tokio-Woodbine section, was discovered on September 4, 1922, by the Natural Gas and Petroleum Company when its Mellor No. 1 was completed. This well produced six hundred barrels of crude per day from between 2,948 and 2,952 feet.

The El Dorado Field was rapidly expanded. By June, 1921, more than one hundred wells had been drilled, and another 340 derricks were under construction. The pool's peak monthly production came in August, 1921, when 1,746,294 barrels of crude flowed from the field's wells. The largest wells in the pool flowed from 5,000 to 10,000 barrels of fluid daily, of which nearly 60 percent was water and emulsion. The largest gas wells produced from thirty million to fifty million cubic feet of natural gas per day.

Pipelines were hurriedly constructed to the area to handle the flow of oil. Standard Oil Company began work on a ten-inch pipeline to join the field with Weller's Station, Louisiana, and the Louisiana Oil and Refining Company was building another line to the area. In addition, the Gulf Oil Corporation tied the field into its pipeline network that carried the crude to its Port Arthur, Texas, refinery. The 10° to 23° Baumé rating of El Dorado crude, however, dropped the price from the expected $0.80 to $1.00 per barrel down to $0.50 to $0.70 per barrel. Nevertheless, development of the field continued, and within a short time the Rock Island Railroad daily was hauling more than four hundred tank cars of crude from the pool. By the summer of 1921, the Gilliland Oil Company and the Shreveport–El Dorado Pipe Line Company were pushing to reach the field, and so much oil was being produced that it was being stored in creeks, ravines, and earthen tanks.

Eventually the El Dorado Field grew to a length of ten miles and a width of two miles—7,740 acres of production. The peak came in 1922 at 10,560,841 barrels before beginning a rapid decline. The field's output dropped to 5,830,000 barrels in 1923 and continued to fall for the next two and one-half decades. By 1947, El Dorado's annual production had plunged to 382,000 barrels. To handle the field's production, T. H. Barton of the Lion Oil & Refining Company and the Root Petroleum Company built large refining facilities at El Dorado. Lion's refinery could handle twenty-two thousand barrels of crude daily, and Root's facility accounted for another twenty thousand barrels every twenty-four hours.

El Dorado, transformed almost overnight from a "quiet rural town with dirt roads reaching back into prosperous farm communities . . . [surrounded] by beech and pine-forested hills . . . [and] peaceful valleys," became one of the wildest boom towns in the

Louisiana and Arkansas oil fields. It was the seat of Union county, and its red brick courthouse was a gathering place for area farmers and their families who flocked to town on Saturdays to sell their produce. Once oil was discovered nearby, however, the town underwent a drastic metamorphosis. "Strangers, keen-eyed and silent," arrived wearing "corduroys, heavy shoes, and leggings."

One of those hoping to find wealth in the Arkansas oil fields was Haroldson Lafayette Hunt, better known as H. L. Born in Illinois in 1889, he left home when he was sixteen and arrived in El Dorado at the height of the oil boom. A poker player, Hunt hurriedly opened a "gambling establishment" but was forced to close its door after a visit from "unfriendly Ku Klux Klansmen." Turning his attention to oil leases, Hunt began speculating on oil property and sinking inexpensive wells. From this modest investment he created one of the world's greatest financial empires.

Another who came to El Dorado was Thomas Harry Barton. Starting the El Dorado Natural Gas Company in 1921, he later opened a small refinery at Doppress south of El Dorado. In 1922 the Lion Oil & Refining Company was organized by several El Dorado citizens. When Barton sold his property to Cities Service, he became president of Lion on January 1, 1929, after first refusing the office, and built it into one of the largest petroleum concerns in the South.

Within a matter of weeks El Dorado's population jumped from approximately four thousand to an estimated fifteen thousand, with more arriving daily. Eventually almost thirty-five thousand people were in the vicinity. At first the local natives marveled as newcomers "trudged through the dense underbrush of ravines and creeks, over the tree-clad hills, or across the pasture lands and farms, looking for 'structure.'" Later the oil prospectors left, and in their place came hordes of oil-field workers with wagonloads of huge timbers, pipes, boilers, and a thousand other pieces of strange-looking machinery. Within days, derricks reared their ugly crowns above the beech and pine forest, and peaceful valleys rang with the sound of banging steel and hissing boilers. Then came oil.

Thousands of camp followers too, flocked to the region intent on making themselves wealthy from the labor of oil-field workers. Prostitutes abounded, liquor flowed freely, and millions of dollars' worth of leases exchanged hands every week. By February, 1921, it was reported that "fully 5,000 strangers are making their headquarters in town," and when the Shreveport Producing and Refining Company's gusher was brought in on March 19, 1921, El Dorado was proclaimed "the youngest gold field in the Mid-Continent Mineral Section."

Leases in the area around El Dorado shot up in value, with one sixty-five-acre tract selling for ten thousand dollars and a one-hundred-acre lease bringing twenty-one thousand dollars. Many local property owners and producers became wealthy overnight. One man, Captain Eugene Constantin, owner of the Constantin Refining Company, which drilled the Hill No. 1, was reported to have retired to an estate at Widville, just outside Paris, France, containing a Louis XIII chateau and 780 acres of cedar forest interspaced with formal gardens. The Garrett Hotel became the center of lease trading activity in El Dorado, and "a person literally had to shoulder his way through the lobby from early in the morning until late at night," one witness recalled. "The people for the most part were trying to make a fast dollar," he continued, and "more wells were drilled in its lobby than in the field."

As all available living space filled up, the Garrett Hotel put cots in its halls, and even the lobby chairs became beds. There still was not enough space, and people walked the streets knocking on doors to beg for a place to rest and offering ten dollars for a night's sleep. Homeowners were asked to rent all available space, and beds were provided for two dollars per night for a single and one dollar per night per sleeper for a double bed shared by two people. Tents were raised and filled with cots, and cheap hotels were hastily constructed. One, the Little Rock Hotel, sported knotted ropes dangling from windows as fire escapes. Fifty men slept in the courthouse, and barber shops rented their chairs for two dollars a night for use as beds. A few men even slept in the Presbyterian cemetery.

Food also was in short supply. Mayor Frank H. Smith and the city council ordered that room on city sidewalks be rented out for eating space. Named "Hamburger Row," this collection of shacks quickly grew to be three blocks long and boasted establishments such as the Jungle Cafe. El Dorado's streets quickly turned to quagmires, and enterprising farmers charged fifty cents to pull vehicles through the mud.

Law enforcement under such conditions became extremely difficult. Arrested criminals first were housed in a large "circus-type" cage in the courthouse yard. Later, a barbed-wire stockade was built behind the courthouse to hold lawbreakers. Guards were on duty day and night, and during bad weather the prisoners were placed in leg irons and housed in the Missouri Pacific Railroad depot. Municipal Judge W. D. Hall levied heavy fines against lawbreakers, and Police Chief Hamp S. Lewis ran any gamblers or prostitutes out of the community. As a result, the undesirables simply moved outside the city limits and reopened for business. Shotgun Valley, near the El Dorado & Wesson Railroad crossing on the route to Magnolia, and Pistol Hill, near the Busey No. 1, were the worst spots. Both were filled with twenty-five-cent dance halls, gambling dens, brothels, and saloons. Another rough community was Upland, about seven miles from El Dorado on the Rock Island Railroad line.

Establishments offering a combination of these vices were called barrelhouses; their bartenders had a practice of placing drunks who had spent all their money inside empty barrels and rolling them out the door. Moonshine sold at $1.25 for a six-ounce soft drink bottle full. Music was generally provided by a three-piece combo of mandolin, guitar, and fiddle. Often, however, only a player piano was available. Some of the better-known establishments were Dago Red's, Smackover Sal's, Dutch's Place, Jake's Place, Big Casino, Cattle Gap, Barrel House Blues, and the Blue Moon. Two-Shot Blondie was a well-known madam and bootlegger, Silvertop was a notorious criminal, and Big Ed was another strong-arm criminal well known to area residents.

El Dorado's Chief Lewis maintained order as best he could. Extra men were hired to control the oil-field workers, a full-time health officer was appointed, and two sanitary officers were employed. In addition, the El Dorado Field's producers helped arrange entertainment. Boxing matches were scheduled, and within a short time an amusement park, which included a swimming pool, picnic grounds, amusement rides, and concessions, was opened. Eventually such efforts drove out the majority of camp followers, and on March 22, 1921, local producers met and organized the Arkansas Independent Oil Producers Association, which did much to clean up the town.

By August, 1921, five refineries and three pipelines were operating out of El Dorado. As early as April of that year, Abner Davis was refining two hundred barrels of crude daily at his facility and selling it to nearby gasoline stations. Crude was selling for about $0.70 a barrel, and by the summer of 1921 there were 275 wells operating in the field. To control overproduction and waste, the Arkansas Conservation Department ruled that all wells had to be located two hundred feet from the lease line and spaced four hundred feet apart on individual leases.

Several refineries, including the Lion facility, a chemical fertilizer plant, a carbon black plant, and three bromine plants were operating in the community. In addition, numerous oil companies, including the Murphy Oil Corporation, the Macmillan Ring-Free Oil Company, the Columbian Carbon Company, and H. H. Cross, established headquarters in the community as El Dorado evolved into the center of the Arkansas petroleum industry.

Although El Dorado rapidly declined in production, the discovery touched off a search for crude throughout Arkansas that led to the discovery of other valuable pools throughout Union, Columbia, Lafayette, Miller, Ouachita, Nevada, and Calhoun counties. But the most important of them all were the great discoveries at Smackover and Magnolia.

Doctor Samuel T. Busey, financier of the discovery well at El Dorado, was honored during an Oil Progress Week observance in El Dorado in his later years. Busey (*second from right*) is being honored by Admiral of the Fleet Chester W. Nimitz (*far right*). *Eunice Spence Collection, Arkansas Oil Heritage Center.*

Left: The huge gas pressures encountered at El Dorado created some spectacular gushers, such as the Barnes No. 1. The drilling crew and visitors gaze at the plume of oil and gas. The drilling contractor for the well, M. Carl Jones of Shreveport, is third from the left. *Estate of M. Carl Jones. Right*: Another massive gusher at El Dorado, the Goodwin No. 2, blew out in February, 1921. Note another gusher in the background to the far right. *Estate of M. Carl Jones.*

At this well in the El Dorado Field the drilling crew posed for the photographer. Note that the derrick floor has been enclosed to afford the workers some protection from the elements. The steam boiler is also enclosed in its own structure, with a "dog run" between it and the well. *Arkansas History Commission.*

At El Dorado, as at many other fields in Arkansas and Louisiana, huge amounts of petroleum were stored in open pits. Production exceeded available means of storage and transportation. Here, oil is being blown under gas pressure into a storage lake near El Dorado in 1923. The crude was being produced by the Umbstead No. 3, owned by the Union Oil Company. *Estate of M. Carl Jones.*

Arkansas oil men operating out of El Dorado, were, *left to right*: Mark G. Wilson, Texota Oil Corporation; Roy M. Sunby; and Jack H. Johnston, drilling contractor. *PennWell Publishing Company.*

A heavy boiler is hauled into the El Dorado Field by a ten-mule team. This was one relatively sure way of getting supplies to the field. When extremely muddy conditions were encountered, the number of mules was doubled. *Graydon F. Smart*, Shreveport Magazine.

Roads that were largely mud bogs often presented major problems in the El Dorado Field. Here, the back wheels of a wagon loaded with lumber are bogged down to the bed of the wagon. The teamsters appear to have little choice but to wait for more mules to help pull through the mud hole. *Ron Shipman Collection, Arkansas Oil Heritage Center.*

Most teaming contractors felt that oxen were more able than mules at pulling extremely heavy loads over difficult terrain and through mud. Consequently, oxen were used throughout southern Arkansas and Louisiana to haul heavy equipment over primitive roads that had become virtually impassable because of rain and the constant passage of heavy equipment. Here, a standard team of ten oxen pulls a heavy steam boiler to an oil-well site near El Dorado. *Estate of M. Carl Jones.*

Teams of mules and "walker" wagons used for hauling supplies to the oil fields near El Dorado. In the background is the blacksmith shop of L. E. Dafter. *Max Taylor Collection, Arkansas Oil Heritage Center.*

Left: Travel by motorized vehicle was extremely difficult throughout much of the El Dorado Field. Motorists wait their turn to be pulled through this mud bog. With tongue in cheek the photographer labeled his photograph, "Have you had this joy?" *Arkansas Oil Heritage Center. Right*: R. E. Buck, sheriff of Union County, Arkansas, in 1928. Sheriff Buck, along with other law enforcement officials in the Arkansas oil fields, had a difficult if not impossible job in attempting to preserve law and order in the wild oil boom towns. *Randolph Allen Collection, Arkansas Oil Heritage Center.*

El Dorado became the headquarters for many of the companies operating in the Arkansas oil fields. With the development of refineries and more permanent jobs in the community, men brought their families to live in that town. The prosperity fostered by petroleum also brought other businessmen with their families to the community. Thus, El Dorado made the transformation from a boom town to a stable community. One of the activities fostered by the increase of family life in the community was the Union County Baby Show held at the YWCA building in El Dorado on October 4, 1923. *Sally Farley Collection, Arkansas Oil Heritage Center.*

A street scene in El Dorado not long after the boom had begun. The street is crowded with automobiles and people. Note the sign on the car in the foreground welcoming new arrivals. *Max Taylor Collection, Arkansas Oil Heritage Center.*

A view of the Union County Courthouse located on the main square of El Dorado, Arkansas, in the mid-1920s. By this time El Dorado had become a substantial, permanent community. *Sally Farley Collection, Arkansas Oil Heritage Center.*

El Dorado became the headquarters city for the Arkansas oil industry, as many of the companies exploiting the oil fields of the region set up offices in the community. Here is an El Dorado street scene near the courthouse in the late 1920s. *Max Taylor Collection, Arkansas Oil Heritage Center.*

The Rock Island Railroad depot at El Dorado, the major departure point for most individuals traveling into the Arkansas oil fields. The most convenient and practical way to go was by rail. *Max Taylor Collection, Arkansas Oil Heritage Center.*

Oil-field workers waiting for the Pine Knot Cannonball, also known as the Roughneck Express. The train hauled workers from El Dorado to the fields in the area between El Dorado and Smackover and on to the north. The train would stop at various places and workers would walk to their jobs. In the evening the workers would catch the train back to El Dorado or wherever they were housed in the field. *Arkansas Oil Heritage Center.*

A 1922 view of the Lion Oil Company's El Dorado refinery. Capable of handling 22,000 barrels of crude daily, the facility was one of several refineries hurriedly constructed in the field shortly after its discovery. *PennWell Publishing Company.*

H. L. Hunt, on the extreme right, was one of the many oil men who traced their fortunes to the strike at Smackover. Hunt parlayed his original leases in the Smackover Field into a multi-billion-dollar empire. *Robert L. Dodson Collection.*

ONE of the greatest discoveries to be made in Arkansas after the El Dorado find was the Smackover Field. Located on Smackover Creek, near the Union-Ouachita county line, Smackover was nothing but a small flag station on the Missouri Pacific Railroad. Wildcatting activity had shifted to the area around Norphlet, eight miles due north of El Dorado, within a short time of the El Dorado find, and at about 8:00 P.M. on May 14, 1922, the Oil Operator's Trust bought in its J. T. Murphy No. 1—discovery well of the Smackover Field. The well was completed to the Nacatoch sand at a depth of approximately 2,024 feet and at a rock pressure of 950 pounds per square inch. Its initial open flow was thirty million cubic feet of natural gas daily, indicative of the tremendous gas deposits that would be found at Smackover.

When the No. 1 J. T. Murphy blew in, the gas pressure was so great that it demolished the derrick and blew out a string of drill stem. The drilling crew fled for their lives as hard-packed red sand was flung high into the air and then rained to earth. People within a quarter of a mile of the Murphy No. 1 had to plug their ears against the roar. A pilot flying over the well at seven thousand feet reported that his aircraft was hit by sand thrown into the air.

Suddenly a crater began to form around the derrick, and despite the best efforts of the crew to save the boiler, it sank into the earth. By the morning of May 15, other craters had begun to form nearby. The escaping gas was ignited by friction, and by that night more than six of them were belching flame. Early on the morning of May 16, the well itself caught fire, shooting flames more than 800 feet into the air. Eventually the craters continued to grow until they formed one huge crater 450 feet in diameter and 50 feet deep. After burning for seven hours, the well put itself out, but periodic gas eruptions continued.

During the holocaust the boiler and drilling rig could be seen "spinning like a top" at the bottom of the crater. One old-timer described the scene: "Why, you could go there and see pieces of that drill equipment boil up, just like sand in a spring. It would boil up and then it would go down. Boil up again and it'd go down. Just bubbling like stew or something boiling." Gas spewed from almost any opening in the ground, and the earth vibrated.

On June 21, 1922, the Oil Operator's Trust completed another well, the Murphy No. 2, one-quarter mile from the Murphy No. 1, in an attempt to relieve the gas pressure, but another crater formed. This one became a "mud volcano" that threw mud high into the air at intervals. Eventually log roads were constructed to the site, and tourists thronged to the wells. Refreshment stands were built to cater to the sightseers.

The field's first oil well was not completed until July 1, 1922, when the V. K. F. Oil Company brought in its Richardson No. 1 on a lease owned by an old-time black camp-meeting preacher, Charles Richardson. Drilled to a depth of between 2,048 feet and 2,066 feet, the well initially flowed at 300 barrels of crude per day. Several other wells were brought in between July, 1922, and April, 1923, but production was relatively small, amounting to between 25 and 150 barrels a day.

Such production attracted many of the Mid-Continent Region's giants. In 1924, W. G. Skelly, one of the region's best-known oil-field operators and the founder of Skelly Oil Company, acquired a large percentage of Smackover's production. However, not until January 28, 1925, when the Lion Oil & Refining Company completed its Graves No. 6, was Smackover's first real gusher brought in. Flowing at one thousand barrels daily from the Graves sand, the Lion Company's well was drilled to a depth of between 2,490 feet and 2,501 feet. Another well, the D. N. Stewart et al. Murphy No. 1, was completed with a production of twenty million cubic feet of gas per day on November 4, 1926.

Eventually the Smackover Field would expand to cover more than forty square miles. The pool was divided into the Louann District (of light oil) in the west, where production was mainly from the Meakin sand, and the Norphlet District (of heavy oil) in the east, where production was mainly from the Nacatoch, Graves, and Blossom sands. The Louann District generally produced 23°–28° Baumé oil, and the Norphlet District basically produced 18°–23° Baumé oil.

Producing crude from the Nacatoch, Meakin, Blossom, and Graves sands and later the Smackover limestone, the pool became the richest of all early Arkansas discoveries. One well, described "as the largest oil well in America," produced twenty-five thousand barrels daily from the Nacatoch sand. So great was its flow that a one-thousand-barrel tank was filled by it in twenty minutes. Other wells producing between five thousand and ten thousand barrels daily were not uncommon.

At the height of its production, Smackover was Arkansas's greatest oil field. Within a year of the completion of the V. K. F.'s Richardson No. 1, more than one thousand wells were being drilled nearby. More than one thousand wells would produce 25,000,000 barrels of crude at Smackover. The field's greatest monthly production came in June, 1924, when its wells pumped 1,182,900 barrels of light oil; eleven months later the field's wells produced 8,201,500 barrels of heavy oil. Smackover's output reached an annual peak in 1925, when 69,000,000 barrels were pumped from the earth. Of this amount, 59,500,000 barrels were heavy oil and 9,500,000 barrels were light oil.

The Gulf Oil Corporation, which had its beginnings in the J. M. Guffey Petroleum Company, the Gulf Refining company of Louisiana, and the Gypsy Oil Company, quickly tied Smackover's wells into its pipeline system, which stretched from Port Arthur, Texas, to Dublin, Indiana. Such a connection opened a vast market for Arkansas crude.

Twelve miles to the east of the Louann District of the Smackover Field, the Stephens Pool (along the Columbia and Ouachita county line) was uncovered in the spring of 1922. Several oil men had attempted to open the area before. S. S. Hunter and his partners, along with the Standard Oil Company, had drilled several wells in the area; one well, the S. S. Hunter et al. No. 1 Lester and Holten, was completed as a small producer at between 2,125 and 2,131 feet on July 16, 1920. It has been claimed as the first authentic show obtained in a well in southern Arkansas, and it did stimulate the search for crude in the region, but not until Hude and Aarnes's Brown No. 1 was completed on June 8, 1922, at a depth of 2,082 feet, was the field opened to production. The discovery well's initial daily production was thirty-three barrels per day of 29.3° Baumé oil.

By 1922 the Stephens Field was flowing at a rate of 28,325 barrels of crude annually; it reached its highest monthly production in August, 1923, when it flowed 88,899 barrels. The field's annual production peaked in 1924 at 787,133 barrels. Nevertheless, the following year, 1925, it was reported that approximately five hundred wells were pumping from the pool. Production from individual wells was generally small, however. Afterward, production declined for many years, reaching a low of 196,000 barrels in both 1939 and 1940. However, production was expanded to 1,485,000 barrels in 1943 and grew to 2,035,000 in 1945. By 1946, Stephens was producing a respectful 1,880,000 barrels per year.

Two other small fields were eventually discovered in the vicinity: the Smart Pool, four miles northeast of Stephens, was opened in December, 1940, and the Wesson Field, three miles east of the Wesson community, was located in September, 1945.

After 1925, Smackover's output began to decline, dropping to approximately 52,063,000 barrels in 1926 and about 35,201,000 barrels the following year. Production later began to fall rapidly. Nevertheless, on January 1, 1930, Smackover had 926 wells flowing at a rate of 5,290 barrels of light oil per day and 2,036 wells producing 41,837 barrels of heavy oil daily. By January 1, 1934, the Smackover Field had produced a total of 315,401,428 barrels of oil. Of this amount, 45,389,875 barrels were light oil and 270,011,553 barrels were heavy oil. By 1946 production had dipped to approximately 4,070,000 barrels.

In 1936, Phillips Petroleum Company sank the first successful well, the Reynolds No. 1, into the Smackover limestone formation. Phillips, which had been founded by Frank and L. E. Phillips in Oklahoma in 1917, was one of the giants in the development of both Arkansas and Louisiana. Drilled in near Snow Hill, the Reynolds No. 1 was completed on May 8, 1936, with an initial production of 180 barrels of oil and 40,000,000 cubic feet of natural gas per day. Topped at 4,897 feet, the Smackover limestone is a porous, permeable Reynolds oolitic limestone zone varying between 100 feet and 300 feet in thickness. Discovery of this deep formation led to the location and development of several other pools called the Smackover limestone fields.

Smackover was well known for its waste of natural gas and oil. The field's huge flow of natural gas was generally burned off by giant torches or simply released into the air. One reporter noted that Smackover was "dotted with lakes of oil, lying at the mercy of the elements." During the summer, the dry weather often cracked the earthen dikes holding the crude and thus allowed it to seep onto nearby ground. Then, during the spring and winter months, heavy rains would wash out the restraining dirt and carry the crude into nearby creeks and bayous. In November, 1922, an estimated one hundred thousand barrels of crude escaped into Smackover Creek from an earthen dike weakened by rains. Lightning also posed a great danger to the exposed crude. It was estimated that 2–8 percent of Smackover's oil production was wasted during the first twelve years of the field's life. Of course the waste of natural gas was even greater. One participant in the boom once counted twenty-five wells blowing wild at the same time in the field.

Because of the great waste at Smackover, Arkansas in 1923 enacted the first of several pieces of legislation designed to end the abuse of natural resources. This law was reinforced in 1927 and 1933. However, just as Arkansas officials were beginning to legislate conservation laws, the federal government began to take a more active role in petroleum regulation during Franklin D. Roosevelt's administration.

Faced with increasing federal involvement, Arkansas Governor Junius M. Futrell quickly accepted the invitation of Oklahoma Governor E. W. Marland to a conference to organize the Interstate Oil Compact Commission in early December, 1934, and in January, 1935, when plans for the IOCC were completed, Jeff Davis and John W. Olvey signed for the state. Any state joining the IOCC was required to enact strict conservation laws, and Arkansas's legislators complied with passage of a comprehensive conservation code in 1939.

That law established the Arkansas Oil and Gas Commission (OGC) as the state's regulatory agency for the petroleum industry. The OGC was empowered to require the plugging of wells to prevent the waste of oil or natural gas; require the filing of logs and drilling reports to show the location of all wells; prevent the drowning by water of any stratum capable of producing oil or gas in paying quantities; require an efficient gas-oil production ratio for wells; prevent "blow outs, caving and seepage"; prevent oil-field fires; identify the ownership of all petroleum-related items; regulate the "shooting" and chemical treatment of wells; prorate the production of various fields; regulate the spacing of wells; and issue various other rules to bring order to the state's oil fields. Two years later, in 1941, Arkansas officially became a member of the Interstate Oil Compact Commission.

Although the find at Smackover resulted in lawmaking by the state, it also caused one of the wildest boom towns in the Arkansas-Louisiana region. Before the oil discovery, Smackover was a small rural community of sixty residents. By November 1, 1922, it had a population of five thousand. Eventually more than twenty thousand people flocked to the find, and, with the exception of St. Louis, Missouri, Smackover had more freight receipts than any other station on the Missouri Pacific Line. Between five thousand and seven thousand letters arrived at the local post office daily, and businesses of every kind "popped up so fast that no record could be kept."

As in most boom towns, the lure of quick wealth brought a horde of camp followers, and law enforcement became a major problem. Tom Gray, Smackover's constable, had only two deputies, so the community decided to incorporate to provide better police protection. Once the proper papers were filed, J. E. Murphy was appointed mayor until an election could be held, but only about thirty-five of the six thousand residents had lived there long enough to qualify as voters. Nonetheless, A. W. Friend was elected to the office, which was quickly passed first to Clayton C. Taylor, then to T. G. Hurley, and finally to Dr. William H. Byrd.

Byrd did his best, also serving as municipal judge. To help finance the new town, he levied heavy fines, often as high as one thousand dollars. Gray continued as constable, wearing two guns while patrolling the town, and was given five deputies to help. Bussey Jones became chief of police. Because of Jones's policy of mounting his men on horses, they became known as the Smackover Mounted Police.

The biggest problems, prostitution and gambling, centered in a collection of barrelhouses, called Death Valley, east of the Missouri Pacific Railroad tracks. There "oil field doves" plied their trade openly during the night and rented horses at one dollar an hour during the day so they could ride among the drilling rigs selling their favors to the crews. Guns were carried openly, and fights were common.

Although roughnecks were warned not to go into Death Valley unless they took four or five men with them, and were well armed, they flocked there anyway. As one old-time oil man recalled, the area was a nest of "honky-tonks, barrelhouses . . . dance halls . . . [and] gambling joints." Most of the establishments had "dance halls up front and in back there were gambling joints, playing poker and shooting dice. . . . It wasn't nothing to have four or five people killed every night." Inside the dance halls the workers paid twenty-five cents to dance with the "ladies." The ladies had apron pockets in their clothes, and the money was quickly dropped there. Once the music stopped, each man was required to pay again.

Other nearby boom towns were Lewis Hill, to the north of Smackover; McKenzie, Laney, Ouachita City, Peanut Hill, Standard Umpsted, Snow Hill, Joyce City, and Miller Bluff to the east; and Norphlet to the southeast.

By late 1922 the law enforcement problem had reached a crisis point, and local residents decided to take matters into their own hands. On the afternoon of November 27, two hundred men dressed in white robes paraded through the town in response to an outbreak of murders. Although the Ku Klux Klan denied it had any connection with the march, the lawless element was warned to leave town or face the consequences. Called the Vigilance Committee, or Saints, the group of oil-field workers remained in existence for a few days. One lawbreaker was killed, several were tarred and feathered, and most of them quickly fled.

Once, after a series of killings at Ouachita City, the Klan was called out in force. Marching into town, the white-robed Klansmen tore down the barrelhouses with axes and sledgehammers, set fire to the debris, and burned the town down. "Everyone that was in there had a gun and we just started to shooting," one participant recalled. "When we got inside that place . . . all the hijackers, bootleggers, and gamblers heard all this commotion and saw all those white robes coming and took to the bushes."

Because there was a severe shortage of housing facilities in Smackover, several companies built camps nearby. One was located near the Methodist Church at Peanut Hill. The church was leased and turned into a dining hall, and a cot house, or big tent, was erected nearby. When the men came into the dining hall, particularly when it had been raining, cold, or sleeting or snowing, they expected good food. If it "didn't look right they would get up on the table and break the table down and throw all the dishes out the window," one Smackover boom participant recalled.

In the middle of the cot house there was a dirt box about ten feet square, and on it was an ordinary oil drum. A gas line was run into the drum, and the gas was ignited to heat the tent. These were not the best accommodations, but they were better than many oil-field workers had. One old-time oil man recalled putting boards across steam boilers and sleeping on the boards to keep warm.

Because of the housing shortage, railroads ran a series of "roughneck specials" from El Dorado into the El Dorado and Smackover fields. The Rock Island Railroad operated trains to Cargile, Smith, Lamberton, Upland, and Catesville before ending at Corine, where the train turned around for a return run. The El Dorado & Wesson ran trains to Oil Hill, where the Constantin and Standard oil companies were operating, and on to Morgan and Newell (Kinard's Crossing). The Missouri Pacific ran two trains a day between El Dorado and Louann, with stops at O'Rears, Gulfdorado, Norphlet, Kenova, Smackover, and Griffin. Often as many as twelve coaches were used on each train to carry the large number of passengers.

Automobiles also were used, but high water at Mathis Mill and Holmes creeks often made the route between El Dorado and Smackover impassable. When the road was open, it sometimes required three hours to make the mud and sand-clogged route. Eventually a jitney bus service was opened between Smackover and El Dorado; the cost of a one-way trip was ten dollars. By August, 1922, four bus trips were scheduled daily.

Enterprising residents often took advantage of the bad roads in the area by clearing paths through the thick forest. Logs were split into rails and used to build corduroy roads; such material was commonly known as "Arkansas gravel." Even so, ox and mule teams were needed to drag boilers and other heavy equipment through the mud, which was so deep in some places that animals bogged down and drowned or suffocated before they could be pulled free. Often the mud was so deep at Smackover that local entrepreneurs built wooden walks across the streets and then charged a fee of fifty cents to cross the knee-deep morass.

The need for large numbers of animals created a great demand for mule skinners, and the intersection of Hillsboro and Washington streets in El Dorado became known as Mule Skinner's Corner. There the heavy hauling jobs were contracted, and good mules sold for between two hundred and three hundred dollars each; worn-out animals brought forty dollars. A team generally included twelve mules or oxen, a driver, his helper, and three skinners. The rent for a four-mule team was fifteen dollars a day, with the driver getting five dollars.

The discovery at Smackover led to the development of twelve other finds in the Smackover limestone area of southwestern Arkansas. Although it would be in the mid-1930s that these fields gained prominence, exploration in the region began much earlier. In early 1921, John F. Magale defined a surface structure in Columbia County near Magnolia, and in 1923 the Mid-States Oil Company drilled a wildcat well there. Several other holes were put down in the same general area, and in December, 1925, the Arkansas Fuel Oil Company completed its F. M. Allen No. 1 in Lafayette County just to the west of Columbia County. The well flowed at twenty barrels per day from the Buckrange sand at the 2,786- to 2,789-foot level. Within a short time five wells had been sunk in the area, but most of the production came from only two of the holes.

Interest in the area around Magnolia was rekindled in 1936 with the discovery of the Glen Rose oil production in the Rodessa Field (just across the state line in far northwestern Louisiana). That same year the Smackover limestone production at Snow Hill was tapped. On March 18, 1937, the Phillips Petroleum Company and the Lion Oil & Refining Company penetrated the Morgan sand horizon at Schuler in Union County, Arkansas. Eventually some fourteen wells were drilled to the Morgan horizon, which covered only about 640 acres of the field.

In September that year the E. M. Jones Marine Oil Company's No. 1 was brought in as a 1,500-barrel-per-day producer from the Jones sand at 7,615 feet. Later, on October 22, 1937, Lion, together with Phillips, completed the No. 1-A Morgan well with an initial daily flow of 720 barrels of condensate from the deep Reynolds oil zone at 7,683 feet. These two wells opened entirely new producing horizons in the Schuler Field and created a small oil boom in the area. By 1939 the Reynolds zone had been expanded to nearly one thousand acres and was being tapped by fifteen wells. Within a short time, the Schuler Field had been unitized, and by January 1, 1942, the pool contained 146 wells spread over four thousand acres. The field's peak production came in 1940: 6,547,000 barrels of crude.

In 1937, the same year production began at Schuler, the Buckner Field was located across the county line to the west in Columbia County, Arkansas. Work on the discovery well, the J. P. McKean No. 1, began in July, 1937, by the Carter Oil Company. In November of that year the bit penetrated the porous Reynolds oolite at the top of the Smackover limestone formation, and the well flowed at ninety-one barrels an hour. Development of the pool was controlled by a forty-acre spacing agreement, and by early 1939 there were ten producing wells in the field.

With these discoveries and new seismic work, Dean A. McGee, chief geologist for Kerlyn Oil Company (the forerunner of Kerr-McGee), became convinced that there was oil in the Magnolia region. McGee had been somewhat involved in Phillips Petroleum's effort in the area when he was with that company, and he quickly persuaded Kerlyn officials to reexamine the country near Magnolia. Under McGee's direction, Kerlyn acquired several leases just east of Magnolia, and Kerr-Lynn & Company, Kerlyn's drilling concern, spudded in the Barnett No. 1 on September 9, 1937, approximately one and one-half miles southeast of a hole drilled by the Mid-States Oil Company and about three-quarters of a mile west of the Elam and Magale failed undertaking. McGee was so involved in the well's progress that he slept in a bedroll in the well's doghouse so he could monitor progress. Later he would postpone his wedding date until the well was completed. Because the region had not previously undergone any intense oil development and was relatively isolated from major shipping points, there were seemingly endless delays. Parts were hard to replace, and supplies were late in arriving. Compounding these problems was the weather. That fall proved extremely wet in south-central Arkansas, and rain and mud caused even more hardships.

McGee hoped to strike the Morgan sands of the Cotton Valley series—the horizon that was producing with such great success at the Schuler Field to the east—at the 6,300-foot level. However, in December, 1937, the drillers reached that depth without finding oil. The hole was deepened to 6,325 feet in the hope that crude was only a few more turns of the bit away, but the effort produced no petroleum.

McGee was greatly disappointed. It had been rumored that should the Barnett No. 1 be a duster, Kerlyn would fold. The situation appeared to be so bleak that the drilling superintendent told the crew, "If you guys can find a job somewhere I recommend you go to it because we don't know whether we can pay you next payday or not." The crew remained.

McGee refused such pessimism. There was oil at Magnolia, and he knew it. To him the solution was simple: acquire additional capital and deepen the well. Additional money was provided by other oil companies with a stake in the Magnolia region, and by the end of 1937 drilling was resumed. Within sixty days McGee's optimism was rewarded. Under his direction the hole was deepened to the Smackover limestone. As the bit penetrated the formation, shows of oil and gas were located in porous oolitic limestone between 7,647 and 7,652 feet and between 7,664 and 7,669 feet. McGee continued to stay at the well site during the deepening of the hole. J. C. Comer recalled the geologist's reaction when the shows of crude appeared: "He scooped up a bunch of it and smelled it. He didn't have to tell nothing. . . . His face lit up like a Christmas tree." They had found oil. Early on the morning of March 5, 1938, the Barnett No. 1 blew in.

Excited by the prospect of a nearby oil boom, local citizens had promised the drilling crew "gifts of hats, shoes, suits of clothes, and royalty interest if they brought in a producer." The oil men were elated when the businessmen began to make good their offers. Local merchants brought gifts of clothing, while nearby farmers offered interest in lease royalties. However, because additional money was needed to complete the well, Kerlyn officials stepped in and convinced all but one farmer to take back their royalty offers and give cash instead.

Prosperity City, an oil boom town, quickly sprang up near the well site. Enterprising entrepreneurs were soon selling hamburgers and soft drinks from hastily constructed stands. Not to be outdone, the drilling crew were buying soft drinks, pouring out the contents, filling the empty bottles with crude from the well, and selling them for fifty cents a bottle. Eventually it was necessary to erect a fence to keep the three hundred to four hundred spectators away from the well site.

The Barnett No. 1 was completed on April 2, 1938, and flowed at a rate of 298 barrels per day through a quarter-inch choke. McGee wanted to market the crude as quickly as possible, and by April 11 he had engaged a contractor to haul the oil to the nearest pipeline connection at El Dorado, thirty-two miles away. Although the Arkansas Oil and Gas Commission restricted production from the Barnett No. 1 to 200 barrels a day until a proration program could be established for the Magnolia Field, the well's output by May 1, 1938, had totaled 8,976 barrels of crude.

After the location of the Magnolia Field, Kerr-McGee went on to become one of the great producers in the Arkansas-Louisiana region and later ushered in the development of the huge offshore reserves by drilling the first well in the open sea out of sight of land. McGee's find at Magnolia proved to be one of the most lucrative and productive discoveries during the late 1930s. After the location of another pool—the Village Field— six miles to the east of the Barnett No. 1, the entire area was developed at a rapid pace. During July, 1938, three additional wells were spudded in on forty-acre plots just north of Kerlyn's discovery well. At the same time, a southwest offshoot was started on the Barnett hole. The first three wells proved to be dry holes, but the offshoot found oil. Realizing that the field lay to the south of the Kerlyn well, oil men began drilling in that direction. Their goal was the Smackover limestone, which generally had an oil column between 178 and 188 feet thick.

The development of the Magnolia Field was orderly because of the work of the Arkansas Oil and Gas Commission. As soon as the pool was located, the commission created rules for its expansion and forced operators to adhere to them. The forty-acre spacing between wells allowed the field to be expanded in quarter-mile sections, which encouraged oil men to postpone drilling until proven development reached their leases. Under such provisions there were seventeen operators active in the field by January, 1941, with a total of 116 producing wells out of 124 holes sunk. Production increased from 68,000 barrels in 1938 to a high of 7,383,000 barrels in 1940; however, the pool's output later declined somewhat.

Magnolia was Arkansas's greatest producer from the Smackover limestone, but the price of reaching the formation was high. The average well was in excess of seven thousand feet deep, and the cost of early exploratory holes was between seventy-five thousand and eighty thousand dollars each. Naturally the price dropped as expansion of the field began on a regular basis, but still the average was between fifty-five thousand and sixty-five thousand dollars per well. Nevertheless, with existing proration orders it was possible for oil men to recoup their cost in twelve to eighteen months.

To McGee and other oil men, this was an acceptable return for their investment, and the field was quickly developed into one of the nation's largest producing areas in the years preceding World War II. Eventually the formation would yield eight oil fields and five gas condensate fields that were significant producers in Columbia, Lafayette, Ouachita, Union, and Miller counties. They were the Atlanta, Big Creek, Buckner, Calhoun, Columbia, Dorcheat-Macedonia, Magnolia, McKamie-Patton, Midway, Mount Holly, Schuler, Texarkana, and Village pools, and to June 30, 1946, their combined output totaled 87,386,000 barrels of crude and 152,192 billion cubic feet of natural gas.

Left: Smackover was the scene of numerous spectacular gushers like this one, the Noe Oil and Gas Company's Workman No. 1. This well flowed initially at an estimated thirty-five thousand barrels per day. *Max Taylor Collection, Arkansas Oil Heritage Center. Right*: Another gusher, the "Burton well," at Smackover. This site, as did most in the area, had to be cleared of thick timber. In this case, just enough area was cleared to build the derrick, as trees almost as tall as the derrick stand close by. *Max Taylor Collection, Arkansas Oil Heritage Center.*

Left: As this view of the Burton well shows, much of the area surrounding Smackover was densely covered with pine and hardwood trees. So close were the trees that the forest often was impenetrable by vehicles. Note the horses tied to the fence in the foreground. In their excitement, the oil men did not bother to unsaddle their mounts. *Robert L. Dodson Collection. Right*: The Oil Operators Trust Murphy No. 1 on fire. This well eventually created an enormous crater that became a tourist attraction. Although the well is a spectacular failure from a production standpoint, it signaled the presence in the Smackover area of tremendous potential reserves of natural gas and crude oil. This photograph was taken at night, and the light from the blaze apparently was bright enough for the photographer to show the surrounding trees and for the sky to be brilliantly lighted. *Ron Shipman Collection, Arkansas Oil Heritage Center.*

A driller poses with some of the equipment on his rig. Note the open chain drives immediately in front of him and to his left. Such exposed chain drives were dangerous, for a man could get caught in them if he became exhausted and careless from working long hours. *Max Taylor Collection, Arkansas Oil Heritage Center.*

A crew of rig builders takes a break from constructing a platform for a derrick. The drilling site was chiseled out of the dense woods in the Smackover area, and logs were used for the foundation of the derrick. *Max Taylor Collection, Arkansas Oil Heritage Center.*

This drilling crew is soaked with oil from a well that has blown wild in the Smackover Field. The well, in the left background, is still gushing. *Sally Farley Collection, Arkansas Oil Heritage Center.*

On the derrick floor of a rotary rig near Smackover. The men are getting ready to screw on a new length of drill pipe. *Max Taylor Collection, Arkansas Oil Heritage Center.*

This drilling crew, at the Bradstreet Laney No. 2 in the Smackover Field, is using cable tools. The cable and the top of the drill bit are visible in the center of the picture. The bull wheel is to the right. The heavy cable around the bull wheel acted as a pulley belt, connected to the power source, probably a steam engine, thus turning the bull wheel and allowing the drill bit to be raised from and lowered into the hole. *Max Taylor Collection, Arkansas Oil Heritage Center.*

Left: The huge output of the Smackover Field quickly overtaxed the extremely limited storage and transportation facilities. Consequently, great amounts of crude oil were stored in open reservoirs. Here, oil is flowing from the Graves Oil Company Ballard No. 1 well into a storage lake. The derrick of the well is in the background. *Max Taylor Collection, Arkansas Oil Heritage Center. Right*: The Arkado Oil Company's Well No. 1 was allowed to blow crude oil into an open-storage lake. A dam was constructed simply at the end of a ravine to create the storage pit. *Ron Shipman Collection, Arkansas Oil Heritage Center.*

On the derrick floor of the Houston Oil Company's Laney No. 4 the flow has been channeled through a gate valve and is being allowed to blow wild to the side of the derrick. *Ron Shipman Collection, Arkansas Oil Heritage Center.*

Oil from the Harry Morris gusher Syndicate No. 3 blowing into a storage pit under gas pressure. *Ron Shipman Collection, Arkansas Oil Heritage Center.*

Left: The Vitek Stringfellow No. 1 blew in at an initial estimated flow of forty thousand barrels per day. An earthen storage tank was constructed to hold the massive flow. *Ron Shipman Collection, Arkansas Oil Heritage Center. Right*: A derrick in the Smackover Field almost completely surrounded by earthen storage pits. *Ted Novick Collection, Arkansas Oil Heritage Center.*

This Dashko and Novick well came in on May 28, 1925, in the Smackover Field at an estimated 27,500 barrels per day. This picture of the well was taken after twenty-two days of steady flow, and on the day of this photograph the well was still providing approximately twenty thousand barrels daily. Pipes transported the production from the well to nearby storage pits. *Ted Novick Collection, Arkansas Oil Heritage Center.*

The McKenzie No. 1 is reflected in a lake of crude. The production of the well far outstripped the storage capability of the small tanks on the far right. *Talmage-Dodson Collection, Arkansas Oil Heritage Center.*

Left: Two oil men use a measuring stick to gauge the crude in a storage tank on a lease near Smack-over. *Talmage-Dodson Collection, Arkansas Oil Heritage Center. Right*: Bill McKenzie became a millionaire overnight during the Smackover oil boom. He attributed his wealth to a seer who had advised him not to sell his land. Fortunately for McKenzie, he followed the seer's advice and became a wealthy man. *Sally Farley Collection, Arkansas Oil Heritage Center.*

Open-pit storage of crude oil continued at Smackover well into the 1930s and 1940s. Here, pipes from several different wells fill a storage lake in the early 1930s. *Phillips Petroleum.*

Phillips Petroleum Company's officials inspect a lake of crude oil being stored in the Smackover Field. Note the derricks above the tree line on the horizon. *Phillips Petroleum.*

A view of a portion of the Smackover Field as it appeared in the mid-1930s. Note the density of derricks on the horizon and the saltwater run from left to right through the middle of the picture. In areas where saltwater from the wells was allowed to flow across the ground, all vegetation died, and many such barren spots remain so to the present. *Phillips Petroleum.*

Teams and wagons loaded with oil-field supplies wait their turn to cross the only bridge over Smackover Creek. When the field boomed, development went forward at a rapid pace, and massive amounts of supplies, equipment, and men were hauled to the fields, thus overtaxing the area's primitive road system. *Max Taylor Collection, Arkansas Oil Heritage Center.*

Oil-well pipe being loaded onto a small boat to float across Smackover Creek. Many wells were located in areas far distant from the only available bridge, and supplies had to be moved across the creek by whatever means possible. Note the oil derrick in the right background on the shore of the creek. The derrick originally may not have been at the water's edge, but it was not uncommon for Smackover Creek to overflow its banks after heavy rains. *Ron Shipman Collection, Arkansas Oil Heritage Center.*

Hauling rig timbers and other supplies to the oil fields near Smackover. The density of such traffic pulverized the dirt roads, making them especially susceptible to becoming quagmires. *Ron Shipman Collection, Arkansas Oil Heritage Center.*

An oil-field supply station in Smackover Field. Stacks of pipe lie in the foreground. *Talmage-Dodson Collection, Arkansas Oil Heritage Center.*

The town of Smackover underwent rapid construction after discovery of oil in the vicinity. This photograph shows a portion of the town being built. Merchants scurried to erect buildings for hotels, cafés, saloons, and all manner of other establishments. A "groceries" sign can be seen already in place on the building in the right center of this photograph, and in the left center a café sign is displayed. *Talmage-Dodson Collection, Arkansas Oil Heritage Center.*

Looking north on the main street of the new boom town of Smackover. *Estate of M. Carl Jones.*

After rains the streets of Smackover soon came to resemble the muddy roads of the oil fields. Here, two mules are pulling an automobile through the quagmire that was the main street of the town. The photographer labeled the combination as a "mulemobile." *Talmage-Dodson Collection, Arkansas Oil Heritage Center.*

Business establishments in Smackover are reflected in the water-filled street. Among the businesses pictured here are the P. A. Griffin Model Variety Store, the Smackover Fruit and Vegetable Company, Goldman's Store, a café, an army surplus store, a hotel, and a drugstore. After heavy rains, the streets of Smackover and the surrounding oil fields were virtually impassable to conventional motorized vehicles. *Ron Shipman Collection, Arkansas Oil Heritage Center.*

A night scene on Broadway Street in Smackover. The Byrd Building on the left housed a number of businesses, including a dentist, a house building contractor, and a café. The building in the middle also featured a café. To its right is the American Theater and on the far right is a pool hall. Note the enormous crowd attempting to get into the café in the Byrd Building and into the pool hall. Proprietors of such successful establishments in boom towns made good money following the oil booms, setting up new businesses as new boom towns were established. In this scene, Broadway Street is a morass of mud and water. *Talmage-Dodson Collection, Arkansas Oil Heritage Center.*

Part of the business district in Smackover in the late 1920s. In the center is Jake's Place, a men's-wear store. To the left of that establishment appears to be an automobile dealership, and in the left background is the headquarters of the American Grocer Company. *Eddy Lewis Collection, Arkansas Oil Heritage Center.*

A scene at the railroad station in Smackover. Traveling to Smackover by rail frequently was the most practical way to arrive at the boom town, given the horrible conditions of the roads in the area. Many oil men lived in El Dorado and rode to work in the various fields by train each day. *Ron Shipman Collection, Arkansas Oil Heritage Center.*

The riverboat *Ouachita* docked at Camden, Arkansas, a boom town in the Smackover Field. The boat was used to haul both supplies and people to the oil fields. Boats like this one were designed to draw twenty-two inches or less of water, allowing them to be used on relatively shallow streams. Riverboat men frequently declared that their boats would "float on a bucket of spit." *Talmage-Dodson Collection, Arkansas Oil Heritage Center.*

Flooding was not uncommon in Smackover oil fields. Here, two men use the most suitable transportation available at Camp New Kennon during one such flood. Note the barracks for the men in the background. Such accommodations, although primitive, often were far superior to what was available in the boom towns. *Talmage-Dodson Collection, Arkansas Oil Heritage Center.*

The interior of a barrelhouse somewhere in the Smackover Field. The bar and barstools are all sawn roughly out of local trees. The roof is sheet metal. Barrelhouses frequently were the scenes of shootings and stabbings, and liquor flowed freely in them. *Max Taylor Collection, Arkansas Oil Heritage Center.*

To combat the rising tide of violence, vice, and crime in southern Arkansas, law-abiding citizens resorted to vigilante action against the numerous gambling dens and other establishments purveying all kinds of vice in the area. This photograph, taken in the Smackover area, apparently is of a group of such citizens displaying their arms and willingness to combat the lawless elements. *Talmage-Dodson Collection, Arkansas Oil Heritage Center.*

An extremely rare view of a Ku Klux Klan meeting at night in Union County, Arkansas, in the 1920s. The excesses of vice and lawlessness that the oil boom towns spawned overwhelmed local law enforcement officials, and local citizens, often roughnecks and other oil-field workers, donned the garb of the Klan to take action against gamblers, hijackers, and other purveyors of vice and violence. Often a group of roughnecks would wear the sheets of the Klan to take revenge on an establishment where a friend or friends had been killed. Such action gave them anonymity, and blame for it was laid at the feet of the Klan. Often it was difficult to determine whether such actions were the sanctioned operations of the Klan or of those working under the guise of Klansmen. *Max Taylor Collection, Arkansas Oil Heritage Center.*

Although on many occasions in the Smackover Field local citizens took vigilante action against the criminal element under the cloak of the Ku Klux Klan's sheets, at other times they acted openly, as apparently is the case here. The photograph was labeled "Smackover's reception committee for hi-jackers." *Max Taylor Collection, Arkansas Oil Heritage Center.*

Here is what the "committee"—a group of vigilantes who were possibly members of the Ku Klux Klan—did to a gambling house at Ouachita City in December, 1922. The photographer labeled the picture "After the Battle of Ouachita. War between Saints and Sinners." Apparently in this case the "saints" won the fight. *Talmage-Dodson Collection, Arkansas Oil Heritage Center.*

The railroad depot at the boom town of Norphlet. Note the great quantity of lumber being unloaded to be hauled to the oil fields for the construction of wooden derricks and perhaps business buildings and housing. The white building in the right center of the picture housed an oil-well supply company. *Max Taylor Collection, Arkansas Oil Heritage Center.*

An oil-well cementing job underway in the Magnolia Field in 1939. Note the large number of cement sacks in the foreground. *PennWell Publishing Company.*

Pipeline workers wrapping a portion of a pipeline in the Magnolia Field in 1926. The line was wrapped with asphalt felt to retard deterioration. *PennWell Publishing Company.*

Left: A drilling rig in the Village Field, Columbia County, Arkansas, in 1938. The producing sand in the area was encountered at depths below seven thousand feet, requiring heavier drilling equipment than had been required in the shallower sands in the 1920s. *PennWell Publishing Company. Right*: The Lion-Phillips No. 1-A Morgan in the Schuler Field. The success of this well in 1938 stimulated considerable drilling activity in the area, and it later was deepened to become a second discovery well in the Reynolds limestone. *PennWell Publishing Company.*

The drilling crew and rig of the discovery well at Schuler, Arkansas, in 1937. *PennWell Publishing Company.*

Development of a major oil field required enormous amounts of cement. Approximately fifteen hundred sacks of cement were stored on this lease in the Schuler Field in 1938. *PennWell Publishing Company.*

The Cities Service petroleum exporting terminal at Saint Rose, Louisiana. This loading terminal was the export point of an enormous quantity of Louisiana petroleum products exported abroad. The operation also included the blending of lubricating oils and the packaging of the product in wooden barrels and tin canisters. The canisters were packaged two to a wooden case for export. *Cities Service.*

LOCATED at the point where Louisiana, Arkansas, and Texas come together, the Rodessa Field in the late 1930s became one of the region's most prolific oil producers. Eventually the pool's productive area included Caddo Parish in Louisiana, Cass and Marion counties in Texas, and Miller County in Arkansas. Exploration in the area began as early as 1910, and during the following fifteen years ten test wells were drilled along the Rodessa Trend. One well, sunk in 1921 by the Latex Community Oil Company, was drilled to the 3,266-foot level before being abandoned. Ironically, it was drilled on the same lease that later would produce the field's discovery well.

Despite the scant production opened by these early wildcat efforts, Dan L. Perkins, a Shreveport geologist, thought the area might yet prove to be a rich field. He carefully studied early logs and discovered a fault running northeast to southwest just southwest of Rodessa. Leasing about six thousand acres along the fissure, Perkins and W. J. Stauffer of New Orleans in the mid-1920s sank a test hole to the 3,003-foot level but abandoned the site as structurally low. Unperturbed, Perkins then turned to the Ohio Oil Company and persuaded it to drill seven wells in the region during 1926 and 1927. Unfortunately, all of them proved to be dusters. Trying again, Perkins contracted with Humble Oil and Refining Company to drill on the lease, but Humble defaulted on the agreement.

Perkins then turned to R. W. Norton, a San Antonio, Texas, oil man, who agreed to join him in a partnership. Previously Norton had been involved in the development of the Pine Island and Homer fields in Louisiana. The two men drilled about twenty wells in the region, all of which proved to be disappointments, before they spudded in the O. J. Hill No. 1 on August 21, 1929, about one hundred yards from the Latex Community Oil Company's well of 1921. Completion of the well took almost a year, but on August 3, 1930, the Hill No. 1 reached the Glen Rose formation of the Trinity group at a depth of 5,509 feet and became the first successful deep gas well in the Shreveport region. Initially the discovery daily produced approximately 11,242,000 cubic feet of wet gas, which contained considerable amounts of light gasoline fractions. Perkins later sold his gas rights to the United Gas Public Service Company.

Rodessa remained primarily a gas field for the next five years, and by 1934 it had become Louisiana's third largest producer of natural gas, with an annual output of 13,934,264,000 cubic feet. However, Norton continued to believe that a substantial pool of crude oil lay beneath the gas; oil men had just not tapped it yet. His persistence was rewarded when, at 10:20 on the morning of July 5, 1935, the United Gas Public Service Young Well No. 1 blew in with a heavy flow of crude from the 6,048-foot level. The well had penetrated the Young sand in the Glen Rose formation.

Located about a mile and a half north of the discovery well, the Young No. 1 touched off a rush to the area. Because of its rapid development, the Rodessa Field was widely known for its waste. Many oil men "ten-spotted" their wells (that is, drilled one well to every ten acres), and because oil was far more valuable than natural gas, the gas often was vented off. Generally the oil-to-gas ratio was approximately one barrel of crude to every ten thousand cubic feet of natural gas. By the fall of 1936, seven hundred million cubic feet of natural gas were being flared daily.

The waste was so flagrant that there was a real danger of the complete depletion of Rodessa's natural gas supply. Finally the Louisiana Conservation Commission stepped in with Order No. 7, which limited the field's gas wells to twelve million cubic feet per day and oil wells to six million cubic feet daily. Eventually this rule stabilized the situation; oil wells were limited to not more than two thousand cubic feet of natural gas per barrel of oil, and the pool became one of Louisiana's greatest producers. Rodessa's output jumped dramatically during the late 1930s. Production rose from 1,364,000 barrels in 1935 to a peak of 19,220,000 barrels in 1936.

In 1935 the Rodessa Field was expanded across the state line into Texas. Although the oil had a satisfactory gasoline content, and production was high (the second well drilled in the Texas portion of the pool flowed at a rate of five hundred barrels of crude per hour), the drilling process was laboriously slow. Often as many as twenty to thirty rock bits and seventy-five days were required to complete a hole. In addition to difficult drilling conditions, there were protests from other East Texas producers about the flush production of the Rodessa Field, which helped depress the price of oil; these Texans were especially incensed that wells on the Louisiana side of the border were given greater allowables. Eventually the Texas Railroad Commission raised the Texas allowable to equal that of adjoining states.

By April, 1936, the Rodessa Field contained 120 wells and sixty-five hundred acres of producing land. However, overproduction became a growing concern. In May, 1936, the field's daily allowable was 350 barrels of crude, but that was reduced the following month to 275 barrels per day. Nonetheless, in 1936 the Louisiana portion of the field produced 19,220,000 barrels of crude, nearly twice the amount produced by the remainder of the state the previous year, and Texas wells added another 3,144,000 barrels.

Overproduction greatly increased in 1937 when the Rodessa's boundaries were extended into Arkansas. The pool's development in that state was even more rapid than it had been in Texas or Louisiana, and that section of the field was quickly riddled by drilling. Arkansas's output from the Rodessa Field was 1,252,000 barrels in 1937, but that amount jumped to 2,317,000 barrels the following year. Cries for relief went up from interested royalty holders and producers alike. Finally, in early 1939, the Arkansas legislature, at the urging of Governor Carl E. Bailey, created a conservation board and brought order to the field.

By 1938 the tri-state Rodessa Field had grown to thirty-five miles in length and four miles in width. More than a thousand wells had been drilled in the field, and nearly 83,000,000 barrels of 43°-gravity and paraffin-based oil had been produced. Production over the next few year continued unabated.

Louisiana's Rodessa production peaked in 1936. That year several of that state's wells in the field were beginning to produce saltwater. Texas' output reached its height in 1937, and Arkansas's in 1938. Afterward, Rodessa's flow of crude began to decline. By 1940 the tri-state field had produced a total of 117,218,985 barrels, but it never regained the prominence it once had held. The field's total output for 1942 was 7,632,000 barrels. The following year, 1943, output dropped to 6,496,000 barrels, and it continued to decrease thereafter.

Early in its petroleum history, Louisiana began to take on the characteristics of a refining center. The key to the state's refinery development was Louisiana's natural access to markets by way of tankers departing from its Gulf Coast ports. In 1909 the Arkansas division of the Prairie Pipe Line Company already had a line stretching through Oklahoma and Kansas to a terminal at Ida in Caddo Parish, Louisiana. One month after its organization in April of that year, Standard Oil of Louisiana began construction of a 270-mile pipeline system from Ida to Baton Rouge. Such a system tied all the production from the great pools in Oklahoma and Kansas to the ocean outlet at Baton Rouge. Once the pipeline was completed, Colonel F. W. Weller of Standard acquired title to a 225-acre tract—a former cotton farm—on the high ground two miles north of Baton Rouge. It was an ideal site for a refinery, as it was bordered on three sides by the railroad lines of the Illinois Central, the Frisco, and the Louisiana Railroad and Navigation Company. By October, 1909, several crude oil stills had been completed, and work was nearing completion on the rest of the project. On November 15, 1909, the facility's first crude stills were charged, and production began at what was to become one of the largest refining centers in the nation.

By 1922 the Atlantic Refining Company had begun refining operations in Louisiana, and in 1928, Louisiana contained 13 of the 143 refineries located in the Mid-Continent–Gulf Coast production area. Although the total number of Lousiana plants ranked fourth behind those of Texas, Oklahoma, and Kansas, the state's refining capacity was 420,100 barrels of crude daily—second only to Texas'. Literally millions of barrels of crude poured into Baton Rouge and another refinery center at Lake Charles through a network of pipelines from Texas, Oklahoma, Kansas, Arkansas, and Louisiana.

Later, in 1938–1939, when Rodessa's huge production flooded the state, Louisiana's total production of crude oil reached 188,065,393 barrels. To that was added the discovery of the Paradis Field in St. Charles Parish by the Texas Company–Louisiana Land and Exploration Company in 1938 and the Eola Field in Avoyelles Parish by Sid Richardson in 1939. Other pools were uncovered at Chalkey and Grand Lake in Cameron Parish in 1938 and 1939, respectively.

To handle the state's ever-increasing production, several modernizations were made at the Baton Rouge refinery complex. Thermal cracking units, which used temperature, pressure, and time to convert the hydrocarbons in the oil, were built to produce high-octane gasoline. Other advances, such as gas absorption plants that recovered light fractions and a hydrogenation process that improved the quality of lubricating oil fractions, greatly increased Louisiana's refining capabilities. In the huge expansion of petroleum production during the war years of the 1940s, Louisiana refineries hurriedly added alkylation process units to produce high-octane alkylate and numerous other advanced petroleum products, especially aviation gasoline. In the postwar years, refining improvements at Baton Rouge included two vacuum pipe stills of 18,500- and 14,500-barrel capacities, used to distill heavy lubricating oils, as well as an atmospheric still; wax and lubricant manufacturing facilities; a polymerization facility, which refined petroleum products without distillation; and several other costly additions.

In addition to the Baton Rouge refinery, two other Standard Oil regional affiliates, the Humble Oil and Refining Company and the Carter Oil Company, were active in the state. Originally organized by Colonel John J. Carter of Titusville, Pennsylvania, the Carter Oil Company was bought by Standard Oil in 1908. The Humble Oil Company had first been organized in 1911 as a Texas corporation and had quickly expanded throughout the Mid-Continent Region. In 1918, Humble's Louisiana production amounted to only about 7,400 barrels; however, by the late 1940s that production had climbed to 8,141,410 barrels annually. Humble had first entered Arkansas in 1921, and by 1925 the company was producing 2,383,278 barrels annually from that state.

With the entry of the United States into World War II, Louisiana's refining capability became even more important. At Lake Charles, Cities Service built an entirely new facility for the war effort at a cost of seventy-six million dollars. In addition to a treating plant, straight-run fractionating, and alkylation, three huge catalytic cracking units formed the nucleus of the facility. Other firms, such as the Tide Water Oil Company, had extensive holdings in Louisiana but shipped their crude by tanker to East Coast refineries for processing.

In 1941 more than 95 percent of East Coast oil supplies arrived there by tanker. Much of the crude came from Louisiana or Arkansas fields by way of the Gulf of Mexico and then up East Coast waterways. With the outbreak of war, even more oil was required, shipments were stepped up, and all privately owned tankers were taken over by the government. The Germans responded by stationing U-boats along the Texas-Louisiana Gulf Coat to disrupt the flow. So bold were the Germans that it was not uncommon for residents along the coast to witness submarine attacks and see tankers burning on the horizon. As one historian recorded, "Visible along the high-water mark for miles . . . after 1942 was a winding black ribbon of oil, and just off-shore lie the hulks which mark the terrible ordeal of the first war year." The losses were not offset until 1944, when the Germans were driven from America's shores.

The losses were so great that alternate methods of getting the crude to the East Coast, either by pipeline or railroads, had to be devised. The federal government spent a total of sixty-six million dollars to accelerate the movement of crude along the inland waterway, and the Plantation Pipeline was laid between Baton Rouge and Greensboro, North Carolina. Completed in December, 1942, it handled 158,000 barrels of oil daily. During World War II additional pipelines, such as the Big Inch and the Little Inch, were laid.

After that conflict ended, oil men began searching for technology that would enable them to explore the one remaining part of Louisiana not yet drilled—the tidelands and offshore.

Left: A crew running surface casing in a well in the Rodessa Field, 1936. *PennWell Publishing Company*. *Right*: A new well in the woods near Rodessa in 1936. *PennWell Publishing Company*.

Left: Conway Baker, a football star at Centenary College at Shreveport, worked as a roughneck on the Young No. 1 in the Rodessa Field. Baker later joined the Shreveport police force. *Pictoral Trade Journal of the Petroleum Industry*. *Right*: This photograph, made in 1941, shows R. W. Norton, discoverer of the Rodessa Field, on the far left. On the far right is I. L. Young, Rodessa storekeeper on whose property the discovery well of the field was drilled. *Pictoral Trade Journal of the Petroleum Industry*.

A large crowd of curious onlookers gathers around the tank of the Haynes Brothers' No. 1 Lawton, the second oil producer in the Rodessa Field, in 1935. *PennWell Publishing Company.*

An Arkansas Louisiana Gas Company gas well head or "Christmas tree" in the Rodessa Field in 1936. *Cities Service.*

Left: Soon after the earliest discoveries, the search for oil and gas moved into the town of Rodessa. Here, derricks are in operation immediately behind a business building in 1936. *PennWell Publishing Company*. *Right*: Derricks became dense throughout the community of Rodessa. In this view they loom immediately behind buildings on the main street of the community. *PennWell Publishing Company*.

Rodessa took on all the characteristics of a typical oil boom town, with hastily constructed buildings and a variety of legitimate and less desirable business establishments. In this photograph, a derrick rears over the Broadway Hotel on the left and Nolen's Cash Store on the right. *PennWell Publishing Company*.

A scene in an oil-well supply lot in the town of Rodessa after a tornado leveled much of the community in the late 1930s. *Mark Stewart and Eugene Spruell.*

Natural gasoline plants were constructed in most of the fields in Louisiana and Arkansas with considerable natural gas production. Natural gasoline, usually referred to as casing-head gasoline before 1920, was made by processing natural gas, and when blended properly with naphtha or kerosene, it was an effective motor fuel. These spheroid tanks of the Arkansas Fuel Company's Rodessa plant were built for storing natural gasoline in 1937. *PennWell Publishing Company.*

Header pipes from both the Louisiana and Texas sides of the Rodessa Field bring gas into the United Gas Public Service Company's eight-thousand-horsepower compressor station, which pumped the gas into high-pressure transmission lines for distribution. The tremendous output of natural gas in the Rodessa Field greatly overtaxed the demand for the fuel, and the price of gas was extremely low. Consequently, enormous quantities of natural gas were flared in the field. Residents of Shreveport could see the orange glow of the Rodessa field at night because of the great amount of gas being burned. *PennWell Publishing Company.*

The huge output of Rodessa and the many other producing areas in Louisiana, combined with the transportation possibilities afforded by the port facilities along the rivers and Gulf coast of the state, stimulated the development of Louisiana as one of the major refining centers in the United States. Each producing area of the state had its refineries. This oil loading rack is at the Superior Refinery in Vivian about 1928. *Jack Norman.*

The Union Refining Company operation between Vivian and Trees City in Caddo Parish. *Jack Norman.*

The Arkansas Fuel Oil Company's Bossier City Refinery as it appeared in 1936. *Cities Service.*

The Arkansas Fuel Oil Company became a subsidiary of Cities Service Oil Company. Here, Cities Service tanker trucks and drivers pose for the photographer at the Bossier City Refinery. *Cities Service.*

A cracking unit at the Bossier City Refinery operated by the Arkansas Fuel Oil Company. The refinery was acquired from the Invincible Oil Company in 1923. The property included 225 acres and a tank farm with a 540,000-barrel storage capacity. By 1925 the refinery capacity exceeded 25,000 barrels per day. *Cities Service.*

New Orleans became an important refining and petroleum shipping center by the late 1920s. This asphalt plant at New Orleans originally handled Mexican and Venezuelan oil with a heavy asphalt base. By 1928 it had started processing West Texas crude. *PennWell Publishing Company.*

A view of Shell Oil Company's Norco, Louisiana, refinery about 1929. The facility was located in St. Charles Parish just west of New Orleans. *American Petroleum Institute.*

Another of the major ancillary industries in the oil business in Louisiana was reconditioning used pipe. Here, men coat pipe at a reconditioning yard at Lake Arthur, Louisiana, for the Pure Creole Pipeline in 1938. *PennWell Publishing Company.*

The port at Baton Rouge on the Mississippi River also became an important center for distributing petroleum products. This tanker is being loaded in 1928 at Baton Rouge. *PennWell Publishing Company.*

During the first years of World War II, German submarine wolf packs operated in the Gulf of Mexico, preying on oil tankers and other ships. This ship, the *Cities Service Empire*, was sunk off the Florida coast by a German submarine on February 22, 1942. *Cities Serivce.*

The Gulf Coast Intracoastal Canal was important to the shipping of petroleum from Louisiana to points east, especially after the outbreak of World War II. This particular tanker, the Texaco 446 designed for use on the canals, had a ten-thousand-barrel capacity and yet drew only eight feet of water. *PennWell Publishing Company.*

The Cities Service Oil Company, as did many other oil companies, responded to the requirements of the war effort in many ways, one of which was the building of a huge refinery complex at Lake Charles, Louisiana. This is the site of the refinery complex, with only a tank farm, before construction began. *Cities Service.*

The Lake Charles refinery as it appeared soon after completion. The refinery was built especially to meet the great demand for aviation fuel on the part of the U.S. Air Force. *Cities Service.*

The audience of workers, family and interested local citizens at the dedication of the Tutwiler Refinery at Lake Charles on May 26, 1944. *Cities Service.*

Cities Service Oil Company executives Temple Tutwiler (*left*) and W. Alton Jones on a tour of the Cities Service Lake Charles refinery in June, 1943. The refinery was named for Mr. Tutwiler. *Cities Service.*

Two major pipelines were built during World War II to move crude oil and refined products from East Texas, Louisiana, and Arkansas to the East Coast. Cities Service executive W. Alton Jones headed the representatives of the oil companies that built these emergency pipelines. The twenty-four-inch crude oil line was known as the Big Inch, and the twenty-inch products line was known as the Little Big Inch. *Cities Service.*

During World War II, many ships of the Louisiana-based tanker fleet were converted to meet wartime needs. The Esso tanker S.S. *New Orleans*, shown here before its conversion, was modified first into a Navy oiler and then into an escort aircraft carrier. *PennWell Publishing Company.*

The Esso *New Orleans*, after its conversion by the Bethlehem Steel Company shipyard into an escort aircraft carrier for the war effort. As a tanker, the 13,500-ton, 552-foot vessel had a rated speed of more than eighteen knots. *PennWell Publishing Company.*

Refining in Louisiana has employed thousands of individuals, including these workmen at Standard Oil's huge Baton Rouge refinery. *Western History Collections, University of Oklahoma.*

Spherical storage tanks at the chemical products section of the Baton Rouge refinery. *Western History Collections, University of Oklahoma.*

A close view of some of the catalytic crackers at the Baton Rouge refinery. *Western History Collections, University of Oklahoma.*

A tanker taking on petroleum products at the Lake Charles refinery's loading facility. *Cities Service.*

A night view of the catalytic cracking units at the Cities Service refinery at Lake Charles. Each of these units processed thirty thousand barrels of crude each day into aviation fuel and other petroleum products. *Cities Service.*

An early close-up of gas boiling the waters in a bayou south of Bourge, Louisiana. Gas seeps were common throughout southern Louisiana, and they were the primary means used by early Louisiana oil men and geologists to locate gas- and oil-producing salt domes. *C. R. Pope.*

ABOUT the time Jennings was drilled, a vast new market for crude was opening up. Shortly after the turn of the century, several major industries in the Gulf Coast region began converting from coal- to oil-powered machinery. The American Brewery Company of Houston and the Star Flour Milling Company of Galveston were among the first. By 1901 they had been joined by the Sunset Brick and Tile Company of Gonzales, the Magnolia Brewery, the Houston Electric Street Railway Company, and the City Brewery of San Antonio. That same year, the Southern Pacific Railroad announced its intention to convert from coal-burning to oil-fired engines. It was quickly followed by the International and Great Northern. Several steamship companies also were making the same conversion. The following year, 1902, the United Fruit Company's S.S. *Breakwater* made a record-breaking trip to South America on oil fuel, and the company announced its plans to convert its other ships to oil-burners.

Many of the major oil companies began a heavy investment in Louisiana in order to be ready to supply the expanding market, while others were founded in hopes of gaining a share of that market. George M. Craig, J. S. Cullinan, and John W. ("Bet-a-Million") Gates helped organize the Producers Oil Company, which soon owned forty-nine thousand acres of leases on the Louisiana-Texas Gulf Coast.

Based on what had happened at Spindletop and Jennings, most oil men believed that the area's salt domes held a vast quantity of petroleum, and all they had to do was to tap that supply. The rush was on, and within a short time oil men were vying for leases throughout southern Louisiana. However, the idea that all salt domes hid a huge pool of oil just waiting to be tapped proved more a dream than a reality.

As early as 1893, oil men had taken an interest in Anse la Butte, a salt dome located about six miles north of Lafayette near Breaux Bridge in St. Martin Parish, Louisiana. That year Charles S. Babin, of Lafayette, was appointed the special agent of Mrs. Emma Pelletier and Honore Breaux to sell, rent, or manage the "mines of coal, oil sulphur, iron, gas, or whatever else may be found" on their property. Babin apparently was successful in attracting Paul Ledanois to bore for crude in the area; however, Ledanois abandoned his hole at a depth of only forty or fifty feet. In 1899 it was reported that two iron pipes were pushed a few feet into the ground near Anse la Butte, and the gas that spewed six to eight feet into the air was ignited to provide light for a local gathering. That same year, A. F. Lucas unsuccessfully attempted to drill an oil well in the Anse la Butte area.

Oil had not been found in paying quantities at Anse la Butte when Spindletop began producing in Texas, but most citizens in the region knew there was gas in the area. In the fall of 1901 the Moresi brothers of Jeanerette, Louisiana, just to the south of Anse la Butte in Iberia Parish, sank a well in the area near the swamp along Bayou Teche; they reached saltwater at the 1,150-foot level. A few months after opening the Jennings Field to production, W. Scott Heywood received several letters telling him of similar gas seeps at Anse la Butte. Intrigued by the possibility of another find, Heywood examined the area, leased several thousand acres nearby, and sent a driller to begin work on a well.

Heywood sank a well on the north side of the swamp near a place where natural gas bubbled to the surface. Although he struck gas at the 1,700-foot level, the extreme fineness of the sand clogged the hole. Heywood then moved his rig to the south side of the swamp but found no sign of oil there. He then moved the drilling equipment back to the original site, bailed the first well, and plugged it back to the 1,170-foot level. Oil gushed 25 feet high as he brought in a hundred-barrel-per-day producer.

The Heywood No. 1, when it was completed, became the first oil well of commercial size producing from beneath an overhang of salt. A salt overhang results when the salt dome is thicker at the top and bottom than in the center. Thus, a bit drilled on the edge of the dome would be likely to strike salt near the top of the dome; then, as it is pushed deeper, it would leave the salt and enter the surrounding formation; still deeper it would reenter the salt. According to the log of the Heywood No. 1, the bit penetrated salt between 268 feet and 540 feet, entered a formation of sand and clay, and then reentered salt. Most early-day oil men believed there might be oil beneath a salt overhang, but this was the first succeful completion of a well proving the idea.

Although Heywood had brought in a producer, wells producing "only" one hundred barrels a day caused little excitement during those early years, and by 1905 the Anse la Butte Field was producing only about nine thousand barrels of crude annually. Not until 1907 did oil men begin serious development of the field. That year, Robert Martin of St. Martinville and Walter Burke of New Iberia, who owned the Lake Oil Company, became interested in the Anse la Butte region and sank a well near Heywood's first effort. On November 14, Lake B. Grow, drilling for the Lake Oil Company, brought in a three-thousand- to four-thousand-barrel-per-day well in the pool, the field's first gusher. Oil men hurried to the strike.

The Gulf Refining Company joined with the Heywood brothers and leased more than five thousand acres in the vicinity. Later, the Gulf Company bought the Heywoods out and gained complete control of the area, but no additional big gushers were discovered. And despite evidence indicating that the Anse la Butte Field was located on an extremely local uplift in which the salt core rose to near the surface, with exceedingly steep local dips immediately about the core, many oil men sank their holes away from the discovery site. Some were as far as three-quarters of a mile from the swamp, and most yielded nothing but saltwater.

Because of their disappointment at not being able to expand the limits of the field, along with the new discovery near Caddo in the northwestern part of the state, most oil men abandoned the Anse la Butte area and moved on. The Lake Oil Company, however, drilled another sixteen producing wells near the discovery hole, most of them within 500 feet of the swamp. Little production was found more than 900 feet from the edge of the water. Some of the field's wells produced huge amounts of natural gas. The Heywood No. 1 spewed water and sand as high as 225 feet into the air, and another Heywood and Guffy well penetrated such a pocket of natural gas at the 800-foot level that the water and sand pouring out of the wellhead buried the machinery under 5 feet of sand.

Although the Anse la Butte Field was relatively small, its production by 1907 had climbed to 76,938 barrels of crude per year, and in 1908, the year following the Lake Oil Company's discoveries, the pool's output reached 219,265 barrels. To handle this flow of crude, a 100,000-barrel earthen tank was built by Gulf Pipe Line Company a mile and one-half east of the field. In addition, several pipelines connected the field's wells to barge or railroad terminals. Anse la Butte's production declined or rose at irregular levels for the next three decades. Beginning in 1940, however, the field's output increased dramatically, peaking at 2,620,000 barrels in 1944.

About thirty miles north of New Iberia, near the junction of the Atchafalaya River and Bayou Bouillon, pioneer Louisiana oil men made another effort to tap the rich petroleum deposits of Louisiana's salt domes. As early as 1902, oil men were probing Bayou Bouillon, which was well known for its natural gas seeps. During the summer that year the Maxwell & Sherwood Company built a wooden derrick on the west bank of the Atchafalaya River near one of the larger gas escapes and began a well on what looked like "a Spindletop-like mount." By the end of July, 1902, the bit had gotten down through the 350-foot level and was in a rock horizon that showed good signs of oil at several places. However, at the 1,562-foot-level no paying quantities of petroleum had been located.

Shortly after the Maxwell & Sherwood effort was abandoned, the Heywood Brothers Oil Corporation started a well near the Maxwell & Sherwood hole. By the end of July, 1902, the Heywood well had penetrated "a stratum ten feet thick, from which was obtained several bucketfuls of oil" before the hole was abandoned.

Several other wells were drilled in the Bayou Bouillon area, but none found petroleum in paying quantities. In 1907, Robert Martin reopened the Heywood Brothers well and at twelve hundred feet reported a show of oil and gas. However, "showings" were all anyone ever found at Bayou Bouillon, and most oil men abandoned the region after the disappointing results.

For many years the inhabitants of Vinton, a station on the Southern Pacific Railroad in Calcasieu Parish, Louisiana, were aware of the region's "sour" gas seeps at nearby salt domes. The discovery of Spindletop Field just across the border in Texas ignited the interest of some area residents. They thought that along the shore of the water-filled sink, or depression, formed by the Vinton salt dome was the most likely place to find oil. The first well drilled in the Vinton area was in 1902 when W. B. Sharp and Ed Prather sank a hole to 280 feet and reported several shows of oil. At about the same time, a well drilled by T. C. Stribling reached a reported depth of 1,000 feet. Stribling's well was the first to discover the area's characteristic feature—a heavy bed of coarse gravel between 400 feet and 500 feet that was almost impossible to penetrate and that contained a heavy flow of black sulfur water. On the positive side, the bit located a show of oil beneath a 22-foot layer of clay, which started at the 101-foot level.

Between 1902 and 1904, six attempts were made to break through the heavy gravel formation. Three of them reached to 1,100 or 1,200 feet. One, the Vinton Oil and Sulphur Company's No. 2 well, struck natural gas at 580 feet. This well also uncovered another problem faced by oil men drilling in the region—the cavernous character of the deeper rock layers. For days the crew of the well reported "no return" for their efforts despite pumping huge quantities of mud into the hole. Another attempt was made in 1907 when Wilkins, Zeizler & Rowson drilled a well at the dome. It was abandoned at 700 feet, the depth where hard rock and gravel were encountered.

Nevertheless, by 1909, eighteen to twenty shallow wells on the east side of the pond were yielding as much as 15 barrels of crude daily. However, the field came into its own in 1910 with the discovery of several flowing oil wells. That year, eleven wells were completed in the pool. All had gotten through the gravel and had punched deep into the salt dome. By 1910 the Vinton Field was producing 26,701 barrels of crude—only a preview of what was to come.

The Vinton Field was the first Gulf Coast salt dome to produce flank oil. In 1911 the Gulf-Wilson No. 1, on the northeast flank of the dome, was pushed to a depth of 2,100 feet, from which it produced 20 barrels of oil daily. Several other wells were sunk along the north and east flanks of the formation, and when their production was added to that of the wells penetrating the core of the salt dome, the pool's output for 1911 amounted to 2,454,000 barrels of crude. Unlike many Louisiana salt domes, Vinton maintained its high rate of production. Promoters in the region were quick to take advantage of this fact; as late as 1918 they were telling potential investors that Vinton was the junction of three great underground streams of oil flowing south from the Arctic Circle. Amazingly, people believed the story.

After dropping to a low of 933,000 barrels in 1912, the pool's output remained in the range of 1,500,000 barrels annually for the next decade. Then in 1923 annual production again broke the 2,000,000-barrel level and remained relatively high until 1935, when it again dropped below 1,000,000 barrels. Yearly production continued to decline for the next eight years, reaching a low of 306,000 barrels in 1940. Then in 1944 the pool rebounded to 1,942,000 barrels, and the following year's production was above the 2,000,000-barrel mark. By 1947 Vinton wells were flowing at a rate of 3,673,000 barrels of crude annually.

A third major field was the Welsh salt dome, located about three miles northwest of Welsh, a town on the Southern Pacific Railroad not far from Jennings. The mound at Welsh, which stood out on the otherwise flat coastal plain, was well known to area residents for its gas seeps. By the summer of 1902, oil men were probing the area. Several wells were drilled by the Texas Company, the Big Mound Oil and Gas Company, and several others, and by 1903 the pool's wells had a total annual output of 25,162 barrels. The next year, the Welsh Field's flow of crude jumped to between 300 and 400 barrels per day from six or seven producing wells, but the total output that year was only 39,892 barrels.

In the early months of 1904 the Welsh Oil and Land Development Company's No. 4 well was brought in as a gusher, which, after it was put to pumping, produced sixty barrels per day for about six months. By 1906, fifteen wells had been sunk in an area roughly fifteen hundred feet square. Although about half the wells proved to be producers, most of them proved to be like the Welsh Oil and Land Development Company's No. 4, which produced steadily for a while and then quit. Very few produced large amounts of crude for any extended period.

Although the Welsh Field did not produce huge amounts of crude, natural gas was found in considerable quantities. Most of the gas was located in the same horizon as the crude, causing oil men endless problems in their attempts to open the pool to production. Several blowouts were reported, and sand gushers—wells that threw plumes of sand into the air as gas roared up the holes—were common sights.

Saltwater was another plague of the Welsh Field. Generally the amount of saltwater pumped was considerably greater than the amount of oil. In addition, the saltwater–crude oil mixture from the field proved difficult and costly to separate at refineries. Most of the field's production was sold to the Southern Pacific Railroad for seventy-five cents to one dollar per barrel. The railroad, which had built a refinery at the town of Welsh, converted the oil into lubricating products for its trains.

During the first six years of its existence, the field averaged only 85 barrels of crude daily—hardly enough to sustain a rush to the area. As a result, there was never a real drilling boom in the field. Only two wells were drilled in 1906, one in 1907, none in 1908, two in 1909, and five in 1910. By the end of the first decade of the twentieth century, a total of twenty-one wells had been completed in the field, seventeen of them producers. Attempts to expand the field from the mound area had been rewarded only by dry holes. As oil men realized that the find was not a major field but a producing area confined to the mound itself, most abandoned the region and moved to more potentially profitable locations.

The Jefferson Island salt dome in Iberia Parish was one of the state's Five (or Fire) Islands, which had attracted oil men for years. Called a variety of names, including Cote

Carline, Dupuy's Island, Miller's Island, Orange Island, and, since 1818, Jefferson Island, it is not a true island but a slight elevation surrounded by marshes. For many years local residents knew of a natural gas seep on the east side of the dome, but it was salt rather than gas that attracted the first drillers. Salt was found at the island in 1894 when a water well struck the mineral at 334 feet. Anthony Lucas later explored the area and sank one well which, when it was abandoned at 2,186 feet, was still in salt. In 1897, eight other wells were drilled, four reaching salt deposits. After that the search was not resumed until 1919, when C. J. Webre drilled thirty-six wells and found nothing but salt. To exploit his find, the Jefferson Island Salt Mining Company was formed, and a salt mine was opened in April, 1923. However, workers in the mine accidentally struck an oil and gas seep, indicating the presence of crude.

In November, 1924, the United Oil and Gas Syndicate undertook an extensive exploration project to find oil and gas on Jefferson Island and nearby Lake Peigneur. Five wells were drilled to a depth of more than 4,000 feet, yet they produced only a show of oil or gas, and the company found itself in financial difficulty. Reorganized as the Jefferson Oil and Development Company, it sank two additional wells but again had nothing positive for its efforts other than a trace of evidence of gas. Afterward the firm reorganized yet again, this time as the Jefferson Lake Oil Company, and another well was drilled. This time a show of oil was found in 73 feet of porous limestone at 1,763 feet, but it was not found in paying quantities, and the project was abandoned.

Unsuccessful exploration had begun years before at the nearby Iowa dome, a deeply buried salt dome about twelve miles east of Lake Charles, Louisiana, in Calcasieu Parish. Exploration in the area began in 1916 when Lee Hager examined several surface gas seeps. In 1923 the Gulf Company, also attracted by the surface gas seeps, drilled a well to 3,381 feet but did not find oil or gas in paying quantities. Three years later, in 1926, the Union Sulphur Company conducted a refraction seismographic examination of the region and sank two holes, one to the 4,850-foot level, just east of the Gulf Company's dry hole. They also were dusters.

Still the area's numerous gas seeps continued to attract oil men. In 1929, Vacuum Oil Company, which merged with the Standard Oil Company of New York in 1931 to form the Socony-Vacuum Oil Company, acquired a block of leases about two and one-half miles south of the Gulf Company's well and two and one-half miles southwest of the Union Sulphur Company's hole. After examining the area, Henry C. Cortes, in charge of Vacuum Oil Company's coastal geological and geophysical work, believed that it contained a deep salt dome. At approximately the same time, the Shell Corporation conducted a seismographic examination of the vicinity, which also indicated a deep salt dome, and acquired another block of leases adjoining the Vacuum Company's tract.

Convinced that there was oil in the deep salt dome, the Vacuum Oil Company spudded in a well on its leases in December, 1930. The bit penetrated 7 feet of Miocene oil sand at the 5,008-foot level, and the well briefly flowed at 4,500 barrels of crude daily before going to water. Encouraged by the find, the Vacuum Company deepened the hole to the 6,971-foot level; there it located an Oligocene sand in October, 1931. The formation proved to be 14 feet of clean oil sand, and the well flowed at 3,180 barrels per day.

Development of the Iowa Field began slowly. In 1932, one full year after completion of the discovery well, the pool produced only 489,000 barrels of oil. However, its output soon climbed rapidly. By 1935 the field's production had jumped to 7,363,000 barrels. Iowa's output then began a decline for the next several years; in 1940 the field's wells pumped only 3,475,000 barrels of oil, and the total was only 2,506,000 barrels in 1942. In the mid-1940s, however, Iowa's output began to climb again, growing to 3,309,000 barrels in 1944, after which another decline began.

Although several salt domes along Louisiana's Gulf Coast were explored by oil men following the opening of the Jennings Field, the findings at first were disappointing. In 1902 the total output of the state's salt domes amounted to 548,617 barrels valued at $188,985. Output continued to increase over the following years until by 1905, Louisiana's salt domes produced 8,910,416 barrels worth $1,601,325. However, only two of the early domes—Anse la Butte and Vinton—were developed into respectable producing pools. Another, Welsh, proved to be a small field, and Bayou Bouillon and Jefferson Island were big failures. Nevertheless, these efforts had attracted the attention of the nation's oil men, and once technology made it possible, the region's flat marshlands were quickly opened to oil development.

As seismography was developed as a tool in exploration, oil men began to explore the vast expanses of marshlands and swamps surrounding southern Louisiana's salt domes. By designing specialized equipment, they overcame the myriad problems involved in drilling in such a hostile environment and uncovered an entire string of oil pools—Golden Meadows, Grand Lake, Hackberry, West Hackberry, East Hackberry, New Iberia, Teppetate, Lafourche, Sweet Lake, Ponchatoula, Gibson, and others—stretching across Calcasieu, Cameron, Jefferson Davis, Acadia, Vermilion, Evangeline, St. Landry, Lafayette, St. Martin, Iberia, St. Mary, Iberville, West Baton Rouge, East Baton Rouge, Assumption, Ascension, Terrebonne, St. James, Lafourche, St. John the Baptist, St. Charles, Jefferson, Orleans, St. Bernard, and Plaquemines parishes. This area, approximately 220 miles wide and 150 miles deep, eventually became the center of Louisiana's petroleum industry.

In 1926, southern Louisiana produced 4,162,817 barrels of crude, or not quite one-sixth of the entire state's output of 23,167,239 barrels. The difference between the two oil-producing regions began to narrow in the late 1920s as oil men tapped the deep deposits of crude found along the flanks of many salt domes. By 1931 the oil production of southern and northern Louisiana stood at 9,661,053 barrels and 11,964,015 barrels, respectively. In the next year southern Louisiana surpassed the northern part of the state in oil output for the first time—10,478,346 barrels, slightly more than one-half of the state's total output of 20,537,476 barrels, as compared to northern Louisiana's total of 9,849,925 barrels. The dominance of southern over northern Louisiana was secured in

November, 1933, when U.S. Secretary of the Interior Harold Ickes set southern Louisiana's proration allotment at 44,528 barrels daily—nearly twice that of northern Louisiana's 24,300 barrels.

This prorationing touched off a great oil boom in southern Louisiana. Throughout the region, as one newspaperman described the scene, "trucks rumble through the streets, restaurants are crowded, hotels are filled and business houses are busy. Out in the network of navigable streams, barges and boats of all descriptions are traveling to and from the marshland fields and seaplanes dot the skies." Thousands of oil-field workers poured into the region. Towns like Houma, New Iberia, Plaquemine, Lafayette, Lake Charles, and Crowley quickly were filled. Once existing living space was overtaxed, many oil companies began building company-owned living quarters in the fields for their workers to overcome the shortage. Some barges were converted into floating bunkhouses. To handle the production, pipelines soon crisscrossed the area through the most difficult terrain, and several local refineries were built. In the absence of adequate facilities for transportation and communication through the marshy land, shortwave radio nets were established to connect the various rigs with supply yards. Generally each field had its own sending and receiving station, and medical aid or badly needed parts could be called for quickly.

The production gap between the northern and southern parts of the state continued to widen over the following years. Southern Louisiana's output grew as advancing technology allowed the full development of the region's vast expanse of swamps and marshlands. The techniques pioneered in this region could not be adapted to offshore drilling, but working in this area did accustom oil men to thinking of searching for oil under extremely trying conditions. By the end of 1946, southern Louisiana contained fifty-two important oil fields, and their total cumulative production, from the discovery of the first major find at Anse la Butte in 1904 to the beginning of 1947, stood in excess of 954,761,858,000 barrels.

The Anse La Butte Field in 1908. Although the first well in the area was drilled in late 1901, the field did not undergo extensive development until 1907. These derricks were located northeast of Flat Lake in St. Martin Parish. *Pictoral Trade Journal of the Petroleum Industry.*

The oldest section of the Anse La Butte Field as it appeared in 1941 when the area underwent new exploration. One of the old wooden derricks on the left contrasts with the new steel derrick on the right. *Pictoral Trade Journal of the Petroleum Industry.*

The Anse La Butte Field was productive over a long period of time. A new section of the field was being drilled in 1941 at greater depths than those of the pool's initial development. *Pictoral Trade Journal of the Petroleum Industry.*

A wildcat well being drilled at the mill of the Joseph Rathborne Lumber Company at Ponchatoula, located in southern Tangipahoa Parish, approximately nine miles south of Hammond and just north-west of Lake Pontchartrain. The well was started on May 9, 1921. *PennWell Publishing Company.*

This crude log raft was used for floating pipe through the LaFourche swamp in 1926. *PennWell Publishing Company.*

Oil men operating in the swamps used a variety of means to transport equipment and supplies to drilling sites. Oxen and mud sleds were often used to haul pipeline material in the LaFourche swamp, where tractors could not go. *PennWell Publishing Company.*

Conditions in the swamps and marshes in southern Louisiana were difficult. This board road was being built through the swamp to the Sorrento Dome in 1928. *PennWell Publishing Company.*

Living conditions in the swamps and marshes in southern Louisiana often were primitive. These Gulf Refining Company employees, photographed in 1928, had relatively luxurious accommodations, using an old lumber camp commissary as a boarding and bunk house. The men, resting during their lunch break, were occupying the only spot of high ground in the swamp. *PennWell Publishing Company.*

The Port Barre Field in St. Landry Parish also required extensive clearing of land for the establishment of drilling operations. This is a view of a portion of that field, which was discovered in 1929. *Louisiana State Library.*

A group of officials of the Pan-American Production Company at the No. 1 Haas & Hierch well in the West Port Barre Field in St. Landry Parish. This was the first well drilled by the newly created producing unit of the Pan-American Petroleum Transport Company, and it was completed as a commercial producer. The muddy conditions required the men to walk on a narrow plank pathway to view the well. *PennWell Publishing Company.*

The Bayou Bouillon Field as it appeared in 1930. Development of the field began as early as 1902. By 1930 the field was completely electrified, that power source being used for both drilling and pumping. *PennWell Publishing Company.*

The superintendents and crew in charge of drilling Union Sulphur Company's No. 762 fee at the Sulphur Dome in Calcasieu Parish. The test well was to be a deep well on the flank of the original dome. *Left to right*: W. M. Petty, driller; John Richardson, general superintendent of production; Drew Collins, field superintendent; Donny Ellender, Bud Carlisle, and Willie Pickard, helpers. *PennWell Publishing Company.*

A portion of the Sulphur Dome Field in Calcasieu Parish, another of the productive coastal salt domes, in 1941. The crude wooden bridge across the water in the foreground was constructed to allow workmen to reach the wells. *PennWell Publishing Company.*

A portion of the interior of a houseboat provided at the Sweet Lake Oil Field for use by Pure Oil Company officials and others who visited the field in 1934. The boat was said to have "every modern facility," including the fancy wood-burning stove in the right foreground. *PennWell Publishing Company.*

The Pure Oil Company's No. 12 Yount Lee, a deep wildcat well drilled at Sweet Lake, Cameron Parish, in 1934. Again, the platform drilling technique was being used. *PennWell Publishing Company.*

Base of operations of the Texas Company on Bayou Terrebonne, twenty-two miles south of Houma, Louisiana. *PennWell Publishing Company.*

The No. 1 Ellender, discovery well of the Lirette Field in Terrebonne Parish, was drilled by the Humble Oil and Refining Company in 1937. It flowed into a storage pit from a depth of 11,615 feet, a particularly deep well for its day. *PennWell Publishing Company.*

The discovery well of the Gibson field in Terrebonne Parish as it appeared in 1937. The well produced from a depth of 9,800 feet. The "Christmas tree" of the well is on the left, and a separator tank is on the right. *PennWell Publishing Company.*

Left: The Fohs Oil Company No. 1 Buckley-Bourg well in Terrebonne Parish. At 13,266 feet, it was the world's deepest producer as of June, 1938. Wells like this one foreshadowed the eventual great production in the 1970s and 1980s from the fabulous Tuscaloosa Trend, which would produce huge quantities of natural gas from below 18,000 feet. *PennWell Publishing Company. Right*: J. L. Kirkpatrick (*left*), superintendent for the Tidewater Oil Company, and Cleaves McDannald, son of A. T. McDannald of Smith and McDannald Drilling Contractors of Houston, at the No. 1 Smedes well near St. Martinville. *PennWell Publishing Company.*

The peculiar properties of the sands in much of Louisiana and Arkansas, combined with high gas pressures, caused many gas wells to blow and then crater. This was the remains of a wild well on the Venice Dome in Plaquemines Parish in southeastern Louisiana. The well blew out from the sand at 240 feet. When this photograph was taken, the crater had filled with water. *PennWell Publishing Company.*

These steel barges are loaded with reconditioned pipe for the Texas Pipeline Company's line from the Lafitte Field in Jefferson Parish. A derrick barge in the background is loading pipe onto the barges. *PennWell Publishing Company.*

A Williams Brothers Pipeline Company barge at work laying pipe in the Lafitte Field in 1937. The company, one of the pioneering firms specializing in construction of pipelines, is now part of the Williams Companies headquartered in Tulsa, Oklahoma. *PennWell Publishing Company.*

The isolation of many of the marsh fields in southern Louisiana led companies to set up radio communications stations. Here, the Texas Company has established a radio communications station in a boat in a lonely area of the Lafitte Field in Jefferson Parish. The boat in the rear was used by the field superintendents. *PennWell Publishing Company.*

The Leesville Field on Bayou LaFourche was one of the most active fields on the Gulf Coast in 1934. The well in the left foreground is the Emerald Petroleum Corporation's No. 1 State, which had just been completed as a good producer. As was typical at other locations on bayous and lakes during this period, barges like those in the left foreground were used for steam boiler setups, fuel storage, and handling of equipment. *PennWell Publishing Company.*

The town of Golden Meadows, located in LaFourche Parish near Bayou LaFourche, saw extensive drilling inside the city limits. Here, derricks rise from the backyards of residents of the community. *PennWell Publishing Company.*

Workmen build foundation forms for a five-hundred-horsepower compressor in the Long Lake Field, LaFourche Parish, in 1938. The compressor, when activated, was used to reintroduce residue gas back into the high-pressure formation from which it was produced as a conservation measure to retain the gas pressure in the field as long as possible. *PennWell Publishing Company.*

These elevated storage tanks were built in an unidentified coastal Louisiana field in 1936. This is another example of the means oil men were required to use to cope with oil production in the swamps and marshes of southern Louisiana. *PennWell Publishing Company.*

The Continental Oil Company's No. 1 Ortego, the discovery well of the Tepetate Field in Acadia Parish, as it appeared in 1935. To the right of the derrick is a two-stage separator designed to separate the crude oil and natural gas being produced by the well. *PennWell Publishing Company.*

M. H. Brown (*left*), tool pusher, and J. D. Poe, driller, both of the Loffland Brothers Drilling Company, pose at the No. 1 Macabees well in the Tepetate Field. The well was drilled for the Continental Oil Company. *PennWell Publishing Company.*

One of the crews of the Carl B. King Drilling Company which drilled the Mills-Bennett Production Company's No. 1 Riverside, a deep wildcat well in Acadia Parish, in 1934. *Left to right*: David L. Harlan, driller; C. Rogers; Dick Bryson; C. E. Goodman; and Joe Gillespey. *PennWell Publishing Company.*

A view of the East Hackberry Field in Cameron Parish in 1936. The barge is being loaded with oil. The East Hackberry Field was particularly notable in that it never had a pipeline, relying entirely on removal of the production by barge. *PennWell Publishing Company.*

The old and the new side by side in 1937 in the West Hackberry Field. On the right is an old wooden derrick, the pump still at work drawing crude from a shallow sand. On the left is a new steel derrick going after deep production. *PennWell Publishing Company.*

The East Hackberry Field extended into Calcasieu Lake. This is a view in 1936 of a recently installed pumping unit barge put in operation on the lake by the Texas Company. *PennWell Publishing Company.*

In many coastal fields it was easier and more economical to power drilling and pumping units by electricity than to use diesel fuel or steam boilers. Here, an electrical pumping unit is in action on a deep well in Calcasieu Lake in 1936. *PennWell Publishing Company.*

A 1940 view of the "Old Hackberry Field," Cameron Parish, where exploration for deep production on the flanks of the original dome was conducted with considerable success. *PennWell Publishing Company.*

Left: This spectacular sight must have been seen on many Louisiana bayous. A floating derrick is being towed down a bayou by tugboat to a new drilling site in 1938. *PennWell Publishing Company.* *Right*: Special barges for laying pipelines under lakes were devised to cope with conditions in Louisiana. This derrick barge, used to lay pipe in Lake Pontchartrain, was being towed to anchor because of a sudden rise of a "swell" on the lake. It was not uncommon for high winds and storms on the lake to cause suspension of these pipelaying operations, which were being conducted in 1941. *PennWell Publishing Company.*

Wild gas wells continued to be a problem in many Louisiana fields well into the 1940s. Here, a special well head is being mounted for transport by truck to tap a wild gasser in the Tepetate Field in 1943. *PennWell Publishing Company.*

Geologists learned to cope with the bayous, marshes, and swamps of southern Louisiana in various ways. In this scene, geophysical survey equipment is being assembled on a barge for a trip into one of the swamp districts in 1935. Note the special high-wheeled wagon on the barge. It was used for transporting seismic equipment in marshy areas. *PennWell Publishing Company.*

A trailer and a special wagon like the one shown in the preceding picture are being towed by mule through a swamp in coastal Louisiana to the site selected by geologists seeking new pools of petroleum. *PennWell Publishing Company.*

Some lake drilling operations were powered by steam boilers. This is a Loffland Brothers Drilling Company boiler barge in use at Grand Lake in Cameron Parish in 1940. *PennWell Publishing Company.*

A Texas Company near-shore drilling operation just off the coast of St. Mary Parish. The photograph was taken from the platform of the completed well in the foreground. *Texaco Archives.*

THE continental shelf lying just off the shores of Louisiana and Texas is an extension of the flat coastal plains of those states. The region gradually slopes from a height of approximately six hundred feet above sea level to a depth of about six hundred feet below sea level. Of varying width—nearly 70 miles at the mouth of the Rio Grande on the Texas-Mexican border and approximately 140 miles at the mouth of the Sabine River on the border between Texas and Louisiana—the offshore portion of this shelf covers an area of almost 200,000 square miles. Of this expanse, the 51,000 square miles which border Texas and Louisiana offer a huge region of prospective salt-dome oil deposits.

Most geologists long had assumed the presence of oil in paying quantities under the coastal waters of the Gulf of Mexico. As early as 1927, David White of the U.S. Geological Survey declared that the salt domes underlying the continental shelf held vast deposits of crude. His was a reasonable assumption. Since the discovery of oil at Spindletop in 1901, more than 556 producing structures had been found on the land portion of the continental shelf, and geologists could see no reason why the salt beds and domes should not extend beyond the coastline. However, the technological problems of getting to the underwater oil, coupled with overproduction and falling prices in the late 1920s and 1930s, prevented oil men from developing the region for many years.

The first efforts at offshore drilling had taken place in California during the late 1890s. Drillers had simply constructed piers from the shore to potential well sites and had operated their rigs from the ends of the piers. By 1908 pier drilling had been adapted in the Gulf Coast area at Goose Creek, Texas, and had quickly spread along the entire southern coastline of the United States. For the next several years pier drilling provided a rich harvest of underwater crude.

The use of drilling platforms in the relatively shallow waters of Caddo Lake by Pyron, Chalk, and Melat was a logical extension of the development of piers. Gulf's use of completely independent piers, which were not connected to the shore, for the drilling of the Ferry Lake No. 1, completed in May, 1911, made it the "world's first . . . true offshore well." Within a short time the idea was adopted by other companies operating in the region. Although drilling platforms in Caddo Lake had proven their adaptability, it would require more than twenty-five years for the idea to be expanded into the Gulf Coast waters.

The next innovation came in 1927 at Huntington Beach, California, where oil men spudded in a well onshore but slanted the hole offshore. This slant drilling quickly became a common practice. Also during the 1920s, several oil companies constructed artificial islands from which they drilled. At the same time, the use of platforms to drill in shallow water came into vogue. Later, in 1933, whipstock tools, which drilled a directional hole by means of a beveled bar placed at the bottom of the hole to deflect the bit, were introduced. All these innovative techniques were quickly adopted by Louisiana oil men and put into practice along the Gulf Coast on the state's inland waterways.

As offshore drilling technology advanced, oil men in the late 1930s and early 1940s began to express a greater interest in the potential of offshore oil deposits. In the early 1930s the Texas Company acquired the rights to a revolutionary submersible drilling barge developed by Louis Giliasso, a retired sea captain. This method allowed drilling equipment to be towed to the well site and anchored in place. Once the well was completed, the equipment was refloated and towed to the next site. This innovation greatly increased shallow offshore exploration in southern Louisiana.

In 1938, Superior Oil Company, in conjunction with the Pure Oil Company, sank a well in 14 feet of water off the coast of Louisiana and struck crude in a salt dome structure at 6,200 feet, just as White had predicted more than a decade earlier. That same year, Humble Oil and Refining Company sank five holes off McFadden Beach in Jefferson County, Texas. These wells were drilled from four platforms in the Gulf of Mexico. Three were connected to the shore by a causeway, but the fourth, nearly a quarter of a mile offshore, was serviced by boats. All five holes proved to be dry.

Not until 1937 was the first drilling structure built in the unprotected waters of the Gulf of Mexico. The platform was constructed by Pure Oil Company and Superior Oil Company south of Creole, Cameron Parish, Louisiana. Located approximately one and one-quarter miles from shore, the well, completed in 1938, was the first in the open waters of the Gulf Coast.

Between 1938 and 1940 the Texas Company embarked on an offshore program in the Coon Point area of Terrebonne Parish, Louisiana. A total of five wells were drilled, but all were dry. After these failures oil men became leery of offshore wells, many regarding them as costly failures.

That attitude, coupled with the outbreak of World War II and accompanying shortages of material and supplies, postponed offshore development until the end of the conflict. Then in May, 1946, Magnolia Petroleum Company began work on a platform approximately ten miles southeast of Eugene Island off Terrebonne Parish. The platform, 77 feet long, 173 feet wide, and 20 feet above the water level, rested on 338 timber and steel pilings, each 110 feet long, driven into the sea bed. Completed after three months of work, the structure was essentially the same offshore design that had always been used by oil men—a design adequate for drilling in protected areas but totally unsuited for work in open waters. Magnolia's effort proved to be a dry hole. Shortly after Magnolia's failure, Louisiana's Creole Field was brought in. Nearly three million barrels of crude were taken from the pool, and interest in offshore wells soared. The result was a boom in platform drilling along the Gulf Coast. Again, however, these efforts took place in protected waters within sight of land.

Kerr-McGee previously had been involved in offshore activity at Mobile Bay and the Mississippi Sound, but Dean A. McGee, head of the firm, had decided the company would have to pioneer an entirely new area of petroleum production—the open sea—if it was to become a major energy concern. McGee was positive that oil could be found in paying quantities offshore; all that was needed was a technological breakthrough that would allow oil men to tap underwater pools. His optimism, however, was not shared by other oil men, many of whom believed that the plan to drill a well out of sight of land in the Gulf of Mexico was extremely foolish.

Nevertheless, McGee was convinced, and in August, 1946, Kerr-McGee acquired from the Louisiana Mineral Lease Board two leases of twenty thousand acres each in the Ship Shoal area off Point au Fer in Terrebonne Parish. Although the leases were in relatively shallow water, they were fifty-four miles from the nearest port and ten to eleven miles from the closest landfall. Out of sight of land, they were located in the open sea with no protection from the storms that periodically swept the area. Tied to these leases was a deadline of September 12, 1947, for the beginning of drilling operations, and by January, 1946, McGee had two seismograph crews searching the area.

Cost predictions for the effort were astounding; the drilling platform alone would cost almost $200,000. Estimates were that it would require fifty days to complete an eleven-thousand-foot well, and during that period all materials would have to be barged to the site. It would cost Kerr-McGee $250 a day just to haul fresh water from the mainland. The total cost of the venture was estimated at more than $350,000.

To ease the financial burden, Kerr-McGee approached Phillips Petroleum and Stanolind Oil and Gas for support. Phillips Petroleum, which as early as 1920 had owned twenty-three thousand acres of leases in Louisiana, had long been active in the development of the Arkansas-Louisiana region, and Stanolind, a fully owned subsidiary of Standard Oil Company of Indiana, was a well-known southwestern oil producer that had taken over the Yount-Lee properties in Louisiana.

Once financial arrangements were made, there was nothing to prevent McGee from ordering the offshore operation to begin. Two wells were to be drilled, one in block 28 and one in block 32, one penetrating to the ten-thousand-foot level and the other to twelve thousand feet. The one remaining problem for Kerr-McGee to overcome was the mechanics of drilling a well in the open sea, with no precedent and where conventional wisdom held it could not be done. McGee turned to a longtime associate, A. T. F. Seale, to help design the necessary equipment. The two had little to work with—no oil field machinery had ever been designed to operate in eighteen feet of water. Before this attempt, all offshore drilling had taken place atop large platforms built on pilings sunk into the ocean bed. Because these structures had to be big enough to hold all the attendant paraphernalia necessary for drilling, they were expensive. To McGee, this was a cost that should be avoided if possible. Under his direction, Kerr-McGee engineers conceived the idea of a platform that would withstand the shock of wave action and that contained the derrick, engine, draw works, and emergency mud tank and pump. The remaining equipment and supplies would be carried on a "floating barge." The barge-platform combination would allow the platform to be salvaged should the well prove to be a dry hole. In such an eventuality, all the Kerr-McGee crew had to do was cut off the piles some six to ten feet beneath the surface, raise the equipment on I-beams, place it on submerged barges, and tow it to another drilling site.

Brown & Root Marine Operators, Inc., received the contract to construct the platforms. The block 32 structure was 38 feet by 71 feet and supported by sixteen steel pilings twenty-four inches in diameter and 140 feet in length. The platform for block 28 was even larger—46 feet by 80 feet. The platforms were designed to rest 20 feet above the sea at low tide, with the rig floor 13 feet higher, where it would be relatively safe from the high winds and heavy seas that frequented the Gulf Coast in hurricane season. The derrick, which rested on the platform, was designed to withstand 125-mile-per-hour winds, and the emergency mud pumps were capable of providing standby emergency facilities for mud operations should the platform be separated from the barge in a storm.

In addition to the platforms, McGee needed some method of transporting the support machinery and equipment used in drilling operations. While the platforms could remain in place as producing centers, the support material should be mobile so that it could be moved from one drilling site to another as need dictated. To solve the problem, Kerr-McGee purchased two surplus Navy freight tenders from the U.S. Maritime Commission for seventy-five thousand dollars each. These vessels had a beam of 48 feet, a length of 260 feet, and a displacement of twenty-five thousand tons. More important, they could easily be modified to serve as combination warehouses, houseboats, and drilling barges.

The key to McGee's plan was the use, for the first time, of a platform in combination with a floating drilling tender barge. This revolutionary innovation not only greatly reduced the expense involved in offshore drilling but also speeded up construction and drilling time. These cost-saving innovations provided the breakthrough that opened offshore drilling.

The barges—which contained enough dry storage area for twelve railroad boxcar loads of drilling mud, chemicals, and cement; a machine shop; a skid-mounted Halliburton cementing unit; and the crew's quarters—were designed to lie alongside the drilling platform parallel to prevailing winds. The workers' compartments accommodated two complete drilling crews. A six-man drilling crew was planned for each tour, with five men to work on the platform and one on the barge to handle the pumps and other equipment. McGee planned for the two crews to work a daily twelve-hour shift until each had worked eighty-four hours. At that time the men would be returned to shore for a week's rest before putting to sea again. In addition to the twelve men who composed a drilling crew, sometimes as many as fifteen others—four seamen, four cooks, two tool pushers, a full-time geologist, a mud engineer, and a drilling superintendent—would be aboard.

Neither the construction of the platforms nor the conversion of the Navy vessels was fully completed when on August 24, 1947, McGee ordered work on the wells to begin. The reason for the rush was the September 12 deadline for starting operations; McGee wanted to avoid the $150,000 penalty for missing the target date. Seismic data had revealed that block 32 overlay a piercement-type salt dome at a shallow depth, while under block 28 was a deep-seated salt dome. Thus, McGee decided to concentrate on block 32, only doing as much as was required by law on block 28.

On September 10, 1947, a scant two days before the deadline, operations began on block 28. A day later, approximately eight miles away, the real effort got underway on block 32. However, within a week a huge hurricane swept the area, forcing the wells' evacuation. Although weather delayed the operation, the men were back on the job by September 19. With no other major problems encountered, work on the planned four-thousand-foot test well progressed rapidly, but the hole never reached that depth. At approximately 9:00 A.M. on November 4, a crew member on the block 32 platform no-ticed that the well's pump was throwing not only mud into the nearby barge but also crude oil. According to Seale, who was watching the crew push the bit through the 1,500- to 1,700-foot level, "We didn't know at first we had encountered oil." When he heard the report of oil covering the barge's mud pits, he rushed to see for himself. Real-izing that it was oil pouring out of the pump, Seale told the tool pusher to skim off the petroleum. By this time the flow was so great that the tool pusher replied, "Skim it off, hell! There's barrels of it."

McGee's discovery was a surprise to everyone, including himself. He had expected to locate crude but had thought it would be at a greater depth. When he learned of the find, McGee told Seale to stop all drilling activity and run an electric log. The results were even more astounding; the log showed that the bit had already penetrated three oil-bearing horizons and one hundred feet of paying sand.

McGee had brought in a nine-hundred-barrel-per-day well and had uncovered a potential one hundred million barrels of new oil reserves. Such production figures caught everyone's attention. Continuing a geological exploration of the offshore salt domes near the well in block 32, McGee estimated there were as many as six hundred acres of production. Even more enticing was the fact that the early seismic exploration of the region had indicated that the most likely spot for crude would be on top of the salt dome at a depth of approximately 3,500 feet, yet a producing well had been brought in some 2,538 feet higher. The find touched off a rush for leases in the area, and by January, 1948, only four months after McGee's discovery, twenty oil companies were hurriedly sinking wells in the open sea off Louisiana's coast, all of them using the technology that McGee had pioneered. A whole new era of oil exploration was opening for Louisiana, the entire Gulf Coast, and continental-shelf regions throughout the world.

Gulf Oil Corporation's No. 3 State, the discovery well of the Timbalier Bay Field in Lafourche Parish. The well is in the process of completion. On the far left is housing for the workers. The Gulf of Mexico is in the background. *PennWell Publishing Company.*

A Texas Company well in the Caillou Island Field, located in the Gulf of Mexico at the entrance of Terrebonne Bay. The tanker ship *Tampico*, to the right, was being used for storage, a practice that became commonplace along the Gulf Coast in the 1930s. *PennWell Publishing Company.*

A Texas Company submersible drilling barge and boiler-house barge in operation at Lake Barre, Terrebonne Parish, in 1934. *PennWell Publishing Company.*

Completed wells in water along coastal Louisiana frequently were protected by piling-supported structures like this one, located in the Lake Barre Field, Terrebonne Parish. *PennWell Publishing Company.*

A Texas Company drilling operation in the coastal waters of Louisiana. The footbridge in the foreground allowed access to the drilling operations and also supported pipelines from the wells. *Texaco Archives.*

Many companies established camps on the water for their workers so they could live near the drilling operations. This Texas Company camp was built in 1934. *PennWell Publishing Company.*

A rotary drilling operation mounted on pilings in the coastal waters of Louisiana. This rig was powered by the steam boilers to the left. *PennWell Publishing Company.*

Steam boilers in Lafourche Parish also were taken to the well site on barges. The tank at the extreme right was for storing boiler fuel. *PennWell Publishing Company.*

Left: A view of a typical 1930s drilling barge, showing pipe racks, derrick, and engine-house floor before the equipment was mounted on it. *PennWell Publishing Company. Right*: A drilling control hookup below the derrick floor on a drilling barge in operation off the Gulf Coast of Louisiana in 1941. *PennWell Publishing Company.*

Providing power to offshore drilling rigs in the 1930s required innovation on the part of the oil companies. One creative response to drilling in this environment was the *Energy*, a power barge used by Texaco to provide electric current to rotary drilling rigs in tidewater locations. The vessel used two Cooper-Bessemer diesel-electric engines of 240 horsepower each to drive electric generators. *PennWell Publishing Company.*

The interior of Texaco's barge *Energy* while it was being used in Terrebonne Parish in 1932 to provide electric power for drilling. *PennWell Publishing Company.*

Getting to the Gulf Refining Company's No. 1 Grandixen in Lafourche Parish required boats like the *Gulf Pride*, upon which the men are sitting. *PennWell Publishing Company.*

By the early 1940s, oil men began using seaplanes as well as boats to reach offshore rigs. *PennWell Publishing Company.*

Left: A plume of water is shot upward by a Kerr-McGee seismographic testing explosion in the Gulf of Mexico in 1945. *Western History Collections, University of Oklahoma. Right*: The tender and platform rig of the Kerr-McGee Oil Company in operation near Eugene Island off the coast of Terrebonne Parish. In 1947, two months after this photograph was taken, the company completed the first successful well in deep water out of sight of land. *Mrs. Claude V. Barrow.*

Kerr-McGee's first offshore well out of sight of land shortly after its completion in 1947. *Western History Collections, University of Oklahoma.*

Six men of the Kerr-McGee Oil Company stand on the rig of the first successful offshore well in 1947. Dean A. McGee is third from left. *Western History Collections, University of Oklahoma.*

A Cities Service seismographic crew on the company's first deep-water offshore effort in the Gulf of Mexico in 1948. That company, in joint ventures with other oil companies, would become especially active in offshore drilling operations. *Cities Service.*

A Cities Service Oil Company crew conducts a seismic shot in the Gulf of Mexico in 1949. *Cities Service.*

With the development of both near-shore and deep offshore drilling, such facilities as this Phillips Petroleum separator and dehydrator became commonplace on properties in the bayou country and offshore in the Gulf. *Phillips Petroleum.*

After Kerr-McGee's first venture offshore in 1947, Louisiana became a center for offshore drilling in the Gulf of Mexico. Here, Shell Oil Company's Rig No. 10 heads to sea past the New Orleans waterfront. Built for economy and easy movement, the rig was specially designed for shallow offshore waters. The converted Navy LST carried a crew of twenty-seven men and rose 175 feet above the waterline. *PennWell Publishing Company.*

A scene typical of many areas of coastal Louisiana. The marshy conditions necessitated construction of the plank road to ensure that workers could reach the drilling rig. *Cities Service.*

THROUGHOUT the early years of the Louisiana and Arkansas oil industry, the two states ranked consistently in the top ten producing states, with Louisiana among the top five after 1930. By the close of the first half of the twentieth century, Louisiana and Arkansas had produced some of America's most productive fields. Smackover, Arkansas, was ranked ninth nationally in total production through 1949, having a cumulative output of 422,758,000 barrels of crude. Caddo Lake in northern Louisiana was in thirty-second place, with a production total of 184,106,000 barrels of oil. The Louisiana portion of the Rodessa Field ranked forty-second in total production during these years, with a cumulative flow of 160,982,000 barrels of petroleum. Haynesville in northern Louisiana produced a cumulative total of 103,136,000 barrels of oil from 1921 through 1949, enough to claim seventy-seventh place in overall rank. And Jennings, on Louisiana's Gulf Coast, ranked eightieth with a cumulative production of 101,012,000 barrels of crude.

Louisiana and Arkansas overlapped into two of America's greatest oil-producing regions. Arkansas and northern Louisiana belonged to the prolific Mid-Continent Region, while the rich onshore and offshore development of coastal Louisiana belonged to the Gulf Coast Region. In 1936 these two regions accounted for 710,898,000 barrels of crude, or 43.16 percent of all the world's oil. That same year of 1936, Louisiana's and Arkansas's combined output of crude amounted to 90,960,000 barrels.

In the years between the opening of the Jennings Field in 1901 and 1947, which saw the completion of the first offshore well out of sight of land, Louisiana produced a total of 1,979,767,000 barrels of crude. Arkansas's output between the opening of El Dorado in 1921 and 1947 amounted to 703,326,000 barrels of oil. The combined total production for the two states from 1901 through 1947 was 2,683,093,000 barrels of crude.

In addition to its huge outpouring of oil during these years, Louisiana became a refining center for both Mid-Continent and Gulf Coast crude. Pipelines connected the state's refineries to pools in Arkansas, Texas, and Oklahoma. Baton Rouge and Lake

Charles became refining centers handling oil from throughout the south-central states. In 1941, four decades after the beginning of the Louisiana oil industry, that state was refining 70,979,000 barrels of crude oil annually. With Arkansas' 12,686,000 barrels for that year, the combined Louisiana and Arkansas refining output totaled 83,665,000 barrels.

Louisiana's Gulf Coast ports and Intracoastal Waterway canals offered oil men access to markets on both the east and west coasts of America and throughout the world. And when Kerr-McGee completed the first offshore well out of sight of land in 1947, an entire new technology was opened to oil men throughout the world. Not only were the rich fields along America's continental shelf now within reach, but undeveloped pools throughout the world also were available. The development of deep-water offshore drilling techniques replaced the need for expensive supply bases ashore with mobile and easily resupplied drilling ships. In the 1970s a new boom came at the Tuscaloosa Trend, continuing Louisiana's prominent place in American oil history.

A barge drilling operation in the Duck Lake Field near Morgan City, Louisiana, in 1952. Oil workers are traveling by boat to reach the rig. *Cities Service.*

The status of Louisiana as a petroleum importing and exporting center continued to grow in the late 1940s and early 1950s. Here, the Cities Service tanker *French Creek* is docked at the Lake Charles Refinery in 1948. *Cities Service.*

Left: W. E. Diamond, derrick man and rotary helper at Bayou Sale, Louisiana, represents the thousands of men and women who have earned their livelihoods by working in some part of the petroleum industry in Louisiana and southern Arkansas. *Western History Collections, University of Oklahoma.* *Right*: A section of the Caddo Oil Field as it appeared in 1955. *Cities Service.*

The Smackover Field has remained productive into the 1980s. This photograph shows a Phillips Petroleum Company thermal secondary recovery project at Smackover in 1964. Steam from generators in the background was injected into the wellhead in the foreground in an attempt to increase production. *Phillips Petroleum.*

A marsh buggy in action. The vehicle's huge hollow wheels enabled it to negotiate the swamps and marshes along Louisiana's Gulf Coast. In water, the wheels gave sufficient buoyancy to enable the vehicle to cross bayous, creeks, and canals. *Interstate Oil Compact Commission.*

Exploration and development of the marsh and bayou oil fields in southern Louisiana continued into the late 1940s and early 1950s. Here, members of a Cities Service seismographic exploration party transfer from trucks to pontoons on their way to a southern Louisiana swamp, where they were conducting a search for oil-bearing formations deep under the swamp's bed. In the background, a tugboat pushes a barge along the intracoastal canal. *Cities Service.*

A tracked marsh buggy and sled used by an Arkansas Fuel Oil Company seismic crew operating in marsh country near New Orleans. Note the boat being towed along behind. *Cities Service.*

Another type of marsh buggy used in South Louisiana in the late 1940s by Cities Serivce Oil Company. *Cities Service.*

Left: An Arkansas Fuel Oil Company crew preparing a seismographic "shot"—explosive charge—to aid in the search for oil and gas in a marsh near New Orleans. *Cities Service. Right*: The shot is detonated in the marsh, and the echoes from underground strata are analyzed for evidence of oil. *Cities Service.*

Oil company personnel began in the early 1950s to use such devices as helicopters and tracked vehicles to search for oil in the Louisiana marsh country. The helicopters, used for getting to seismic operations and well sites, provided savings in both time and money. *Phillips Petroleum.*

Pipelining along the Gulf Coast carried with it unique problems, among them the ever-present difficulties of water and mud. Here, a pipeline crew is preparing to lay a pre-bent section of pipe across a small bayou. *Interstate Oil Compact Commission.*

Kerr-McGee Rig No. 54 being towed under a bridge in the fog at New Orleans in 1963. Spectacular sights like this became fairly commonplace to citizens of southern Louisiana as offshore development continued to the present. *Western History Collections, University of Oklahoma.*

Left: As offshore oil development has continued, fishing in many of the areas has actually improved because platforms became eco-centers for various types of fish. Here, a member of a drilling crew takes time to wet a line. *Cities Service. Right*: Louisiana's oil history may be just beginning. Here, a drilling barge probes twenty thousand feet into the Tuscaloosa Trend searching for natural gas in 1980. The Tuscaloosa Trend in southern Louisiana has proved to be one of the United States' most significant energy provinces, containing huge reserves of natural gas. *Phillips Petroleum.*

Oil and gas operations have touched the lives of most residents of Louisiana either directly or indirectly. Students at Louisiana State University, Baton Rouge, got a first-hand view of operations when this well was drilled on campus in the early 1950s. *Louisiana State Library.*

Bibliography

Unpublished Materials

"Brief History of Texaco Inc. in the State of Louisiana." Archives, Texaco Inc., New Orleans, Louisiana.

Hayes, Thomas D. "History of Petroleum in Southwestern Louisiana, Discovery and Early Industrial Development." M.A. thesis, University of Southwestern Louisiana, Lafayette, 1971.

Jones, Marshall. "Speech Made before the North Louisiana Historical Association, January, 1981, Oil City, Louisiana."

McGee, Dean A. "Recent Developments in Offshore Drilling, Gulf Coast." Archives, Kerr-McGee Corporation, Oklahoma City, Oklahoma.

Newspapers

Daily Tribune. El Dorado, Arkansas.
Oil and Gas Journal. Tulsa, Oklahoma.
Smackover Journal. Smackover, Arkansas.
Wall Street Journal. New York, New York.
Times Picayune. New Orleans, Louisiana.

Published Materials

American Petroleum Institute. *Petroleum Facts and Figures, 1950*. 9th ed. New York: American Petroleum Institute, 1951.

Arkansas Statutes, 1947. 5 vols. New York: Bobbs-Merrill Company, Inc., 1948.

Attaway, Don. "Trees, La.—State's First Oil Field Town," *Shreveport Magazine*, December, 1977, pp. 22, 40–42.

Barton, Donald C. and George Sawtelle (eds.). *Gulf Coast Oil Fields*. Tulsa: The American Association of Petroleum Geologists, 1936.

Beaton, Kendall. *Enterprise in Oil: A History of Shell in the United States*. New York: Appleton-Century-Crofts, Inc., 1957.

Bell, H. W., and R. A. Cattell. *The Monroe Gas Field, Ouachita, Morehouse, and Union Parishes Louisiana*. Louisiana Department of Conservation Bulletin No. 9. New Orleans: Louisiana Printing Company, Ltd., 1921.

Boone, Lalia Phipps. *The Petroleum Dictionary*. Norman: University of Oklahoma Press, 1952.

Buckalew, A. R., and R. B. Buckalew. "The Discovery of Oil in South Arkansas, 1920–1924," *The Arkansas Historical Quarterly* 33, no. 3 (Autumn, 1974): 195–238.

Clark, J. Stanley. *The Oil Century from the Drake Well to the Conservation Era*. Norman: University of Oklahoma Press, 1958.

Coignet, G. O. (comp.). *A List of Louisiana Oil and Gas Fields and Salt Domes Including the Offshore Areas*. N.p.: Department of Conservation, Louisiana Geological Survey, 1967.

"The El Dorado–Smackover Saga," *The Arkansas Lawyer* 7, no. 2 (March, 1973): 66–82.

Ezell, John S. *Innovations in Energy: The Story of Kerr-McGee*. Norman: University of Oklahoma Press, 1979.

Fancher, George H., and Donald K. MacKay. *Secondary Recovery of Petroleum in Arkansas: A Survey*. A Report to the 56th General Assembly of the State of Arkansas. El Dorado: Arkansas Oil and Gas Commission, 1946.

Fenneman, N. M. *Oil Fields of the Texas-Louisiana Gulf Coastal Plain*. U.S. Geological Survey Bulletin No. 282. Washington, D.C.: Government Printing Office, 1906.

Forbes, Gerald. *Flush Production: The Epic of Oil in the Gulf-Southwest*. Norman: University of Oklahoma Press, 1942.

––––––. "A History of Caddo Oil and Gas Field," *Louisiana Historical Quarterly* 29 (January, 1946): 59–72.

––––––. "Jennings, First Louisiana Salt Dome Pool," *Louisiana Historical Quarterly* 29 (April, 1946): 496–509.

Franks, Kenny A. *The Oklahoma Petroleum Industry*. Norman: University of Oklahoma Press, 1980.

––––––, Paul F. Lambert, and Carl N. Tyson. *Early Oklahoma Oil: A Photographic History, 1859–1936*. College Station: Texas A&M University Press, 1981.

Harris, G. D. *Oil and Gas in Louisiana, With a Brief Summary of Their Occurrence in Adjacent States*. U.S. Geological Survey Bulletin No. 429. Washington, D.C.: Government Printing Office, 1910.

Heithecker, R. E. *Engineering Studies and Results of Acid Treatment of Wells, Zwolle Oil Field, Sabine Parish, La*. Washington, D.C.: U.S. Bureau of Mines, 1934.

Knowles, Ruth Sheldon. *The Greatest Gamblers: The Epic of American Oil Exploration*. Norman: University of Oklahoma Press, 1978.

Louisiana Library Commission. *Louisiana: A Guide to the State*. St. Clair Shores, Mich.: Scholarly Press, Inc., 1976.

Matson, George C. *The Caddo Oil and Gas Field, Louisiana and Texas*. U.S. Geological Survey Bulletin No. 619. Washington, D.C.: Government Printing Office, 1916.

––––––, and O. B. Hopkins. "The De Soto–Red River Oil and Gas Field, Louisiana." In *Contributions to Economic Geology (Short Papers and Preliminary Reports), 1917*. U.S. Geological Survey Bulletin No. 661. Washington, D.C.: Government Printing Office, 1918.

Nehring, Richard. *The Discovery of Significant Oil and Gas Fields in the United States*. 2 vols. Santa Monica, Calif.: The Rand Corporation, 1981.

Neville, Louisiana, High School. *Monroyan, 1933*. Archives, Ouachita Parish Public Library, Monroe, Louisiana.

Rister, Carl Coke. *Oil! Titan of the Southwest*. Norman: University of Oklahoma Press, 1949.

Ross, J. S. "Deep Sand Development in Cotton Valley Field, Webster Parish, Louisiana," *Bulletin of the American Association of Petroleum Geologists* 14, part 2 (January–December, 1930): 983–995.

Ruffin, Tom. "The Birth of Offshore Drilling," *Shreveport Magazine*, August, 1975, pp. 17–19, 73–75.

Schneider, G. W. "Urania Oil Field, LaSalle, Winn, and Grant Parishes, Louisiana." In *Structure of Typical American Oil Fields: A Symposium on the Relation of Oil Accumulation to Structure*, I, 91–104. Tulsa: American Association of Petroleum Geologists, 1929.

Scott, W. W., and Ben K. Stroud. *The Haynesville Oil Field, Claiborne Parish, Louisiana*. Louisiana Department of Conservation Bulletin No. 11. Shreveport, La.: Castle Printing Company, 1922.

Shannon, Pierce. "When Drilling Goes Out to Sea," *Drilling*, April, 1948, pp. 36–37.

Spooner, W. C. *Oil and Gas Geology of the Gulf Coastal Plain in Arkansas*. Arkansas Geological Survey Bulletin No. 2. Little Rock, Ark.: Parke-Harper Printing Co., 1935.

———. "Homer Oil Field, Claiborne Parish, Louisiana." In *Structure of Typical American Oil Fields: A Symposium on the Relation of Oil Accumulation to Structure*, II, 196–228. Tulsa: American Association of Petroleum Geologists, 1929.

Stipe, Jack C. (ed.). *Salt Domes of South Louisiana*. New Orleans: New Orleans Geological Society, 1960.

Struth, H. J. *The Petroleum Data Book, 1947*. Dallas: Petroleum Engineer Publishing Co., 1947.

Sundt, Olaf F. "Recent Developments in Gravity Prospecting on Gulf Coast," *Bulletin of the American Association of Petroleum Geologists* 19 (January, 1935): 1–24.

Teas, L. P. "Cameron Meadows and Iowa, Two New Coastal Louisiana Fields," *Bulletin of the American Association of Petroleum Geologists* 16 (March, 1932): 255–257.

West's Louisiana Statutes Annotated. 28 vols. St. Paul, Minn.: West Publishing Co., 1975.

Williamson, Harold F.; Ralph L. Andreano; Arnold R. Daum; and Gilbert C. Klose. *The American Petroleum Industry*. 2 vols. Evanston, Ill.: Northwestern University press, 1963.

Winham, H. F. "An Engineering Study of the Magnolia Field in Arkansas," *Transactions of the American Institute of Mining and Metallurgical Engineering*, Vol. 151, *Petroleum Development and Technology*. York, Pa.: The Maple Press, 1943.

York, Exa. "The Birth of the Oil Industry in Louisiana," *Acadiana Profile* 6, no. 4 (1978): 69–71.